The Death of the Church and Spirituality Reborn

What is the Point of a Religion?

The Death of
the Church and
Spirituality Reborn

What is the Point of a Religion?

Reverend John Littlewood

CHRISTIAN
ALTERNATIVE

Winchester, UK
Washington, USA

First published by Christian Alternative Books, 2017
Christian Alternative Books is an imprint of John Hunt Publishing Ltd.,
Laurel House, Station Approach,
Alresford, Hants, SO24 9JH, UK
office1@jhpbooks.net
www.johnhuntpublishing.com
www.christian-alternative.com

For distributor details and how to order please visit the 'Ordering' section on our website.

Text copyright: John Littlewood 2016

ISBN: 978 1 78535 541 7
978 1 78535 542 4 (ebook)
Library of Congress Control Number: 2016944521

A CIP catalogue record for this book is available from the British Library.

Design: Stuart Davies

Printed and bound by CPI Group (UK) Ltd, Croydon, CR0 4YY, UK

We operate a distinctive and ethical publishing philosophy in all
areas of our business, from our global network of authors to
production and worldwide distribution.

CONTENTS

I would like to dedicate this book to two people, Sue, who is my counselling supervisor, and Dendle, who is my spiritual mentor. Each in their own way challenged me to clarify my ideas and put them down on paper to share. Together they declared I needed a platform for my voice to be heard. So blame them if you think it should be silenced!

Also by Reverend John
The Way – A Celtic Qabalah

About the Author

The Reverend John Littlewood has a science background with a degree in Mathematics and Physics although he studied theology at Ridley Hall, Cambridge, is an ordained Anglican priest and a past university lecturer in counselling with Exeter University Extramural Studies. He has also been a Diocesan Exorcist, is a psychic and a therapeutic counsellor. He runs a charity and counselling agency in Cornwall, UK. In the 1970s he was a parish priest for 5 years but left the parish ministry to concentrate on remedial counselling.

He hastens to point out that he is not a parish priest any more, although he did serve two curacies in the remote past and is presently Licensed to the Truro diocese, however, the saying is that the eunuch is probably the most knowledgeable expert of life and technique within the harem despite his obvious inability to perform! So what does that make Rev John?

His other works include the published book *The Way – A Celtic Qabalah*, a modern approach of looking at the different interpretations and reinterpretations over the centuries of the profound mystical symbol, to delve beneath the presented symbols that are held in these various frameworks and to try to understand the basic principles of the Qabalah itself. It is a set of images that is not dependent upon the past or borrowed from any religious setting other than from these Isles. It is essentially a workbook. It presents a system to develop self-awareness, to provide a therapeutic framework, to be seen as a mystical and magical pathway and a widening of understanding of all things spiritual and religious. It is not an idle read. You really have to work on the exercises in order to keep up, for this is not a parlour game. It is serious stuff.

Introduction

Some jottings by a priest, past his sell-by date, that are reflections on the deplorable state of the Church of England and spirituality generally in the UK.

It was not intended to be an intellectual or academic work but more a musing of the rapid changes over the last 50 years of church life. It became something else. Despite the rather profound depth of investigation of spirituality the author tries to use everyday words where possible and only falls into 'church-speak' now and again. It is an attempt to clarify trends that are leading to the death of the Church and an attempt to bridge the gaps between incompatible religious bedfellows. Above all it shows a desire for a more spiritual approach to the pastoral care of the nation.

The series begins with a Rant but progresses to some disturbing ideas. It is controversial and will upset people from the more orthodox faiths as well as individuals ploughing their lone furrow. However, it makes some very serious practical suggestions to bring about positive change.

Any Bible references are taken from the New English Bible.

What is the point of a religion – any religion?

And if God truly guides the Church as claimed, then where is He taking it?

Part I

The Death of the Church

1

'Messy Church'

The Church is very much in decline.

No matter how loudly some church members – especially those at diocesan level – pronounce to the contrary, it is vanishing down society's plug hole at an ever increasing rate. It has become an irrelevance to most ordinary people and its voice has lost its power to proclaim to the nation. Nowadays it is perfectly in order to discriminate against the Christian and mock his or her stance but it is a dangerous affair to pick holes in Islam.

"But it is vibrant in so many city centres! There are more young people than ever before making commitment! Weddings have never been so popular! Remembrance day is always packed!" and so on and so on. However, the statistics speak louder than words, for when I was first ordained in the mid 1970s there were about 25,000 stipendiary clergy – all male – licensed in the Church of England throughout the country, but today in the mid 2010s there are possibly less than 6,000 both male and female together. Without the leadership the membership must suffer, and a corollary of a reduced leadership and membership together means that the pool for replacing retiring clergy is consequently reduced. The appalling conclusion is that at some point in the past this inevitably led to a corresponding decline of quality of leadership – including the non-reducing hierarchical positions! It is a spiralling situation with really only one conclusion. That speaks volumes.

There has been so much 'navel gazing' over the last 50 years or so. Possibly it was motivated by the sudden decline of attendance at Evensong when the Forsythe Saga was first screened on BBC TV on a Sunday evening. However, there swiftly followed liturgical revision 'ad nauseam' with various rites and Prayer Books offered as incentives of meaningful worship for young newcomers. Ordination of women was a hot potato at one time and that has finalised with the acceptance of woman bishops voted in only recently by Synod. Theologically I have no issue with the ordination of women, although I need to expand that in my last essay, but indeed at many a diocesan meeting there are more female dog collars than male floating around and I have heard it said that the church is becoming a female group meeting where a man is out of place, generally feels emasculated and so disinclined to participate further.

I can see how this came about, for with less and less money to pay full-time clergymen, there has been more and more reliance upon non-stipendiary clergy, and it is a noticeable feature in the Alternative Therapy and Spirituality scene that women and retired men are likely to predominate. They are usually the ones not dependent upon earning a living in this manner – much to the ire of men and women who do – and who have turned an interest or hobby into 'a calling' to take up a caring or pastoral role. Obviously the Church takes advantage of such unpaid labourers but it would seem that the result was generally not something that was particularly admired initially by the body of believers.

Any society or group of people without leadership will decline, and it doesn't take a financial genius to see that there is a financial watershed that once passed means the remaining church members cannot support the increasing financial burden of buildings' upkeep, diocesan expenses and clergy salaries. Where the Church Commissioners were the unknown and unseen benefactors holding the shadowy purse strings in years gone by who saw to that side of things, now the clarion call is for a greater giving by those remaining in the flock to stop the rot or turn the tide, for the Church is running out of money and simply cannot support its stipendiary workforce and high maintenance buildings. Fewer and fewer people are being asked to give even more money than ever before. It is a situation of ever decreasing circles that cannot continue for much longer.

The customary practice in most dioceses has been to combine parishes, to rationalise or 'consolidate' the situation and spread the butter ever more thinly. The problem of that is there comes a time when the spread butter is so thin that it loses its flavour and effectiveness. The traditional roles of evangelism and pastoral care is defeated by the exponential increase of administration, committees and meetings, meetings and yet more meetings. The general populace no longer knows how to respond to a parson or consider seeking one out for pastoral help these days. In fact there is usually no parson living for miles around anyhow.

Surely the church is past that watershed of financial collapse for even supposing that there be sufficient clergy waiting in the theological college wings to enter upon the parochial stage (and there most certainly isn't) there is still no money to pay them, and without replacing the clerical leadership, despite the non-stipendiary sticky plaster resolve, the church has collectively buried its head in the sand and denied there being a problem.

That, to my way of thinking, is a far better understanding of 'Messy Church' than what is advertised outside many a church building these days, and what is the Church doing to get out of such a mess? Is there a way back from eventual extinction and becoming just an interesting historical cul-de-sac of religious practice? The last fifty years has seen a monumental decline of the Church within society. I truly doubt if it will last another fifty years. My plea is to revise the priority of present day ministry and recall the whole point of a religion before wasting the remaining resources on a proven black hole of irrelevance in today's mainly secular society.

2

What is the Point of a Religion – any religion?

Just what is the point of a religion – any religion, I ask?

One rather cynical reply is that it is a means to keep control of the masses. Another, a bit more positive, is that it is a civilising force down the centuries, bringing Law and Order, Justice and Peace instead of anarchy and mayhem. But when you consider all the religious wars that have taken place, the murder, pillage and torment down the ages, all in the name of religion or God, the very least you can do is wonder what God thinks of it all!!

During Medieval times the Christians brought barbaric bloodshed to the Holy Land through the Crusades. Those atrocities reverberate down the centuries and have been mentioned today to justify the 9/11 and the London bombings – although I agree that might be too simplistic a comment. But there has been over 400 years of bloodshed in Northern Ireland between Christian Protestant and Christian Catholic – and the existing peace is so fragile at the moment. There has been conflict for over 3,000 years between Jew and Arab in the Middle East which shows no ending in sight. The Inquisition brought utter terror throughout parts of Europe. There have been the witch hunts; burnings of people on both sides during the Reformation; the wholesale slaughter of Druids and Pagans in the UK and the expunction of the Cathars in France. The list can continue on and on.

On a much smaller scale religion provides the theatre of power play and jealous manipulation and back stabbing in every parish. I have been a parish priest so I have been there, done that and got the T-shirt! It goes on at such things as PCC meetings, in the Flower Guilds, choirs and Synod meetings. You cannot pretend it does not happen to some extent *everywhere* – it does – because we are all human with all the weaknesses and frailties that humanity brings.

So perhaps, like me, you sometimes wonder what the point of it all is. Perhaps the world would in fact be a better place without any religion in it! So let us pretend what might happen if tonight, on the point of midnight, every religion and every trace of religion vanished. No churches, no mosques, no temples, no Bibles, no Koran, no theological works of any kind, no priests, no Imams, no Holy Men or Women, no evidence of any kind of continuing religious influence remaining. What might happen?

Then tomorrow there might be a walker on Dartmoor watching the dawn come up and with a sense of wonder and awe feel also frustrated and at a loss because he or she cannot find the concepts or words to express that wonder. There is nothing there!

Or perhaps at a local hospital, on the maternity ward, a young mother holds a newborn baby up to her husband or partner and together they delight and share the most intimate moment of the miracle of new life created between them, but then find they cannot really communicate the depth of feeling or wonder or awe at the mystery of new life that is presented there. They do not have the concepts, words or understanding to convey those feelings.

Or perhaps an old man is holding the hand of his wife, a wife of 50 years plus who is gradually dying. And as they look at each other in love they find they do not have the concepts, words or means of giving comfort to the other with a shared hope of what is to come.

I somehow think that by the end of the day a thousand new religions would have been started; religions that come about as people try to share their experiences, finding greater significance in the sharing with like-minded people and in the sharing find a greater facility of understanding – new religions are born. It is evident that there is something hard-wired in the human psyche that requires an acknowledgement of something greater than self that most people acknowledge to some extent or other, even though there is a tiny minority who would love to dismiss such a claim.

I am not a parish priest, although I was one about 30 years ago. My ministry has been one of counselling, and I am the Administrator of a counselling agency. So when a person comes to me who is confused, distressed and feeling overwhelmed by problems or a horrendous situation, then it is no good me telling them to pull their socks up, forget everything and get on with life. That does not work. Things would have long gone past that stage. Yet you cannot just pretend that the bad or sourness does not exist for they are causing such distress. So you have to gently – but firmly – help that person to look at the negative or painful situations – not run away from them; accept all the nasty feelings of anger, jealousy or hatred as well as the more positive ones of love, compassion and wanting to get through the pain, all in order to find a better understanding of what is truly happening and sort out the fantasy from fact. And it is only then that you can also help them to find resources and strengths to cope with the fears and darkness, to work through the situation and grow stronger and wiser as a result. *That is the point of counselling.*

So let me return to religions and worshipping communities, for the same thought processes exist in counselling.

As a member of a worshipping community, it is no use to simply pretend that the bad or sourness does not exist. Of course it does. It is no good to say to a person who has been stabbed in the back by other members of the community, metaphorically speaking, or discovered that their child has been abused by their parish priest, or a relative blown up by a terrorist bomb, to say "turn the other cheek and forgive" or a religious cliché such as "smile because God loves you" and hope those awful emotions and thoughts will go away! That will not work. People who have been so terribly hurt will be livid and want justice – justifiably so.

Those negative feelings and thoughts of jealousy, pain or even revenge will be present no matter how much others tell such people to forgive and forget. Pain and negativity will get in the way of truth, fellowship and communion with each other and God. They need to be explored, accepted and understood – just like in counselling – because they are part of a person's humanity; accepted and owned before any action can be taken. That is why, instead of counselling sessions, there are sermons, Lent and Advent courses, Alpha courses, Confirmation classes and Sunday Schools. That is why in the practice of the Christian religion there is Confession, Absolution, Penance and Forgiveness, Sanctification and Spiritual growth. And in the complete privacy and honesty that is present within our minds during prayer, for God knows the darkest secrets of our hearts, then a person's humanity can be owned or embraced with all its frailty and weakness. It is only then that a person can see how much of an impact hurt and pain can have on their soul or 'psyche'. It is only then that forgiveness may be discovered and spirituality may stand a chance to become more apparent. Spirituality may grow and the people grow in faith despite and through the pain and suffering – or in Christian terms, to come through from personal crucifixion to personal resurrection – to spiritually grow. *THAT is the point of a religion.*

A religion – any religion – if it is to have any worth, is not an intellectual exercise. It is not a thought experiment. If it was then it is no more than a philosophical debatable issue. A religion is an experiential phenomenon. It is to help express the inexpressible; to accept the paradoxes of the mysterious; to find ways of under-standing this thing called 'spiritual' or appreciate the presence of something great and wonderful about a place or person that can grow in that appreciation and influence – and the reverse of that in perceiving the essence of wrongfulness, curses and evil; to find some kind of relationship with that presence that most people understand as God and God's ways.

If that is not foremost then the religion has lost its way!!!

No matter how high sounding or important a cause or issue may be it must still be secondary to matters spiritual for that religion. Even if the cause is a just and prodigious struggle against cruelty, poverty, misuse of political power, abuse, slavery, paedophilia, or one thousand and one just causes to crusade about – even an evangelistic zeal to promulgate that religion, it is still a *consequence* of spirituality. It is but a response to that communion or atonement or awareness of God. Of course a religious person may fight the good fight, but that should never be the prime motivation for that person. The fight is a secondary response and a consequence of the primary experience of relating in some way to God.

So how does the good old C of E rate on that issue?

3

There is only one God - and 'XXX' is God's name

I am sure you must have had it said to you as a form of challenge, 'Why are there so many different religions when you are all worshipping the same God? Why don't you all get together, put your differences aside and stop fighting each other?'

At first hearing that is an inescapably sane and sensible statement to all rationally thinking people. But of course it is not as simple as that. I only wish it were!

One timeworn picture to illustrate that above statement is the one of a mountain with various routes to the top and to God. One route is where the Christians are climbing; another is slightly around the corner and so not visible to the Christians but that is where the Buddhists are climbing; yet further round is where the Jews are climbing, and so on and so on. Each route is distinct and clearly marked, at least to begin with, but although all are climbing upwards there is no communication or sight of the others. The conclusion is that eventually the individuals en route are able to acknowledge there is only one God but just different routes and understandings to attain the presence of God.

Not so!!

There may be a mountain route labelled 'Christian', for example, but two things become clearer the higher you are on that route. One is that the higher you are the more lonely you become as more and more fellow Christians fall by the wayside. The other is that the view becomes wider and clearer. The outcome of the latter is you begin to see other mountains and other people climbing them. In fact the higher you climb the more certain you are that these other climbers – be they followers of Islam, Buddhists, New Agers or whoever – will never meet one another, despite their respective climbs upward to God.

The reasoning is simple in that the different mountains represent different religions and so the end result of each religion is different. The spiritual goal or growing spirituality for each adherent or follower is different. Let me write further by looking at the 'Big Five'.

I am in very great danger of oversimplifying and doing each of the five main religions a terrible disservice, but allowing me rather a lot of leeway you can see their respective spiritualities are not the same. They may overlap and have common elements, but they are essentially different.

So for example, the goal of the followers of Islam is to know and accept the Will of God, with that phrase often quoted as a means of accepting an uncomfortable outcome. For the majority the Will of God is to live in harmony and peace with all people even should it be something of a struggle. But there is the built in trap to such a view of being fatalistic and simply accepting what is happening as if that is what *should* be happening, for that must surely be the Will of God.

Some followers of Islam see things in a very different light and understand the Will of God as being that all peoples should be followers of Islam, even if it means violence and possible suicide to bring this about. To truly know that Will of God and submit to it will be rewarded in an afterlife of great comfort and satisfaction, but to know the Will of God is not an easy thing to achieve. It is an arduous climb.

For a Jew the Will of God is more black and white, for it is to obey the Commandments of God, especially as interpreted in the Talmud. In this case the end result or spiritual goal is to proclaim to the world that the Jews are the Chosen Ones of God and for them to live their lives accordingly. They are a royal priesthood to the nations. They are an elite. Their very lives are examples or a call to the nations to convert. It is a form of evangelism that the Christian will sympathise with.

11

That, of course, does not sit well with the other nations or other religions and is a constant sore spot with their neighbours, hence it is another arduous – but spectacularly different – climb. However, like the followers of Islam the Jew will be richly rewarded for such constancy in an afterlife.

The Buddhist route appears almost as a non-religion to many. Unlike Islam or Judaism, which are religions formed by interpreting real live events that gradually reveal the nature of God in an ever changing society, Buddhism is more a philosophy that calls for a certain way of living. The Buddhist believes in Reincarnation, and through endeavours to follow the 'Middle Way' seeks to rise above earthly passions and appetites and enter the state of mind or state of blessedness called Nirvana. In this state there is no need to reincarnate, but unfortunately this is usually achieved through a high degree of suffering and denial of the body's needs. The end result is that at the end of that present incarnation the soul will 'merge with the Cosmic Consciousness' that lies beyond the individual's understanding of 'self'.

The Hindu way is almost opposite to the Buddhist! Like Buddhism, though, this eastern religion accepts the basic tenet of belief in reincarnation, but unlike Buddhism the end result of getting off the wheel of reincarnation is by experiencing as fully as possible all that it means to being a human being. In other words each incarnation is to be fully embraced to experience life as that person in its entirety, and each incarnation will be as a person in a different walk or position of life. So a thief must experience what it fully means to be a thief; a prince should immerse himself in prince-hood; a princess similarly; an artist similarly; and so on and so on. The Hindu way is to embrace Life, and the spiritual goal is attained through a procession of lives that encompass the totality of human experience that is embarked upon by every soul and will take millennia to achieve.

The Christian religion is different yet again and although it arose from the Jewish 'root', it is quite different from Judaism and can be stated in the most simple terms, in that Christian spirituality is about growing Christ-like. Notice it is not about giving a tithe of income, following set rules or acknowledging certain days of the year, giving up anything, praying unceasing, nor to become a missionary, bishop or great anything. It is not about declaring a Christian catechism, creed or evangelical jingle. A Christian may be any of these or do any of these things, but the point to Christianity is that a Christian is such because he or she identifies with Christ – puts 'on' Christ – has faith in Christ – accepts the Spirit of Christ – or however it might be spoken of. That, of course, can lead to one's own kind of crucifixion and if this is not first and foremost then the rest of the package is of no spiritual value within the religious package.

Unfortunately to my way of thinking, if the 'Spirit of Christ' were to disappear from the Church of England I wonder if anyone would notice!

4

God made a mistake!

Did you know that there are several forms of established Christianity? And I am not talking about sects or denominations here.

When Vasco De Gama discovered the sea route to India in 1497, the Christian sailors did not recognise the Christian religion of those lands. It was so foreign an expression. It did not have the same scriptures, style of buildings, institutions or stories or 'hymns'. For them, it could not be Christianity. However, the Church of South East India had been started through the evangelism of Saint Thomas, the Doubter. He had travelled east whilst Paul and Peter had gone west to Rome. It is obvious to us today, with hindsight, that the fledgling church in India would have arisen naturally from the people and customs of that place, using things which were meaningful to them. It could not have been otherwise. They used their Indian concepts to express the 'new truth' – hence a very different resulting Church developed.

Two forms of Christianity came to Britain. There was the Roman form that travelled from Rome through Gaul (modern day France) across the Channel to Kent and centred itself at Canterbury in the South East of the island. There was also the Celtic form that started in the deserts of the Holy Land, developed and grew along the North African shore, travelled with the pirates of those lands to Ireland, blossomed in Ireland and eventually crossed the Irish Sea to Northern England, Scotland, Wales and Cornwall.

The two were quite different, for just as the Indian Church developed out of the Indian culture of the time, so these two grew in separate and divergent ways. The Roman Church's expression was one of Empire. It saw the political strength, power, expansionism and sway that the Roman Empire had over the surrounding lands, and the Church of Rome reflected this. It became an evangelising expansionist church. It developed political skills, political partners and gradual social dominance and it would not be cowed despite persecution and martyrdom. There were divisions ultimately within it, divisions we now know of as Catholic, Protestant, Reformed, Episcopalian, Lutheran, etc., but all these sprung from the same root and have essentially the same basic concept of the need to spread the gospel and bring in the kingdom of God here on earth as understood by the Church.

The Celtic expression had started in the quietness and emptiness of desert life rather than the bustle of empire. Living in the desert meant that a person was aware of mystery, quietness and the fragility of life, to wonder at the stars and celestial cycles, to be aware of where water was to be found and its miraculous power over life, of plants with healing properties or their power to kill, of reading the signs within Nature to work with it or die, and the church reflected this. It was not a church that particularly sought dominance or power but was a quiet expression of understanding of the necessities of life amid the cycles of life, death and rebirth. It thrived on solitude, meditation, listening, prayer and observation both in the religious sense of services and in the sense of awareness and service to all God's creatures. It was the more obviously heavenly minded or otherworldly of the two, being far more at home in the unseen and subtle world than its politically more astute counterpart ever did.

The Celtic language was a spoken language and not essentially a written one. The only script in any kind of use was the Ogham script, consisting of clumsy runes and truly hard going, often carved onto sticks and stored as bundles, rather than inscribed on scrolls of vellum as was the Latin or later Saxon. Recorded in the Ogham script as a necessity were not the stories of the Celtic Saints and ways of the Church but the laws and government protocols of the Irish. These showed such a high order that their Roman cousins of the time appeared barbaric and uncivilised. Inheritance and power were not the prerogative of the male and Justice did not rely on might or chance. The Celtic Christianity had had immeasurable influence on the social mores of the time, but indirectly. It worked by working 'with the social flow' rather than producing the flow by itself. It showed by example rather than diktat or subjugation.

The two expressions clashed in Britain. Their agendas were different, their motives and modus operandi were different, and they even had different calendars. One *had* to give way to the other and no prizes given to guessing which one would dominate. It was an inevitable outcome, but in my humble view I want to believe it was the wrong one! Did God get it wrong?

5

What was there before Christianity in these lands?

What of the religion in these lands before *any* kind of Christianity arrived? Well certainly Druidism was present and so was a form of Wicca or the Old Religion, both steeped in the use and understanding of the 'unseen'. In fact in all probability these two religious expressions were the two wings of the same original bird. If I have got it right, the history – the law (or lore) and storytelling – were more the prerogative of the male priesthood, while healing, fecundity and intuition were more under the authority of the female priestesses or wise women. The pre-Christian religion of these lands had essentially split over the centuries, giving birth to these (apparently) two separate religious expressions by the time the Romans were on the scene. Neither of them stood a chance during the Pax Romana which made possible the wave of incoming Christianity of both the Roman and Celtic kinds, although the Roman expression certainly was more powerful and successful than the Celtic in the evangelism of the time. In fact I believe the time was right for a new religious expression to emerge throughout the lands anyhow, as the old had held sway for many a century. The religious scene needed revitalising with new blood.

With the incoming tide of political reform or power politics of the expanding Roman Empire throughout the Celtic countries, the old order – with its own religions – was swept away. Profound reformation took effect. Probably any new religion would have done the trick, but just as it was a politically expedient move by Emperor Constantine to embrace Christianity and 'establish' it as the empire's religion, so it was Christianity that appeared on the scene as part of the Roman world, and would inevitably decry the Old Religion.

In the most general terms, if one country is trying to dominate or subdue another then the points or foci that rebellion centres upon are strong leaders, strong national identity and the nation's religion. I know it is commonsense but from those three foci hang all endeavours, both for and against domination. Usually the strong leaders are either executed, exiled, imprisoned or they go underground. The strong national identity is virtually impossible to overcome, so it is generally ignored and continually ridiculed or belittled over the years. It is hoped that eventually the sense of identity weakens, but even so this may prove inadequate. This was seen upon the re-emergence of the various states that had made up the USSR and Yugoslavian states and even the re-emergence of the state of Israel in the 1940s. The Middle East is in an utter turmoil of political shifts and there is much concern about the self-styled Islamic State with its echoes of the Ottoman Empire.

Religion, however, is a slightly different issue, and looking at the examples from history we can see three prongs of attack that constitute a 'Take Over' process.

The first involves the least effort and applies to just about any and all takeovers. The conquering nation brings in its own religion and belittles the existing one. Because the new country has succeeded in its takeover then the existing old religion's Gods have proved inadequate to the task of defending their host nation. They must be weaker than the new country's Gods, so for everybody's sake leave the old and embrace the new. One example of this is seen in America where the Native American shamanism took a major knock and the Bible Belt grew as a consequence. I know this example could be considered simplistic, but another example is Elijah battling with the old religion of the Philistine priests of Baal, or the Christian Evangelism sweeping over the African continent in the wake of Imperialism. In England, Morris Men have been laughed at and the old religion declared as really nothing more than superstition.

If that is insufficient then the action 'hots up'. If the practices and ideas of the old religion are proving too stubborn to eradicate then they are incorporated into the new. The propaganda or spin is that "you almost got it right, but in fact we also have these same ideas and Gods but in a new and improved form". Hence festivals such as Christmas, Easter and so many of the Saints' days are reinvented, whilst the worship sites are rededicated to the new improved version of the God. The populace has no focus to its rebellion for its focus is now the new religion, practice or worship site. That is just good psychology. This is seen not only in the Christian religion taking over the Wiccan or Old Pagan worship in the UK, using new saints etc. that closely resembled the old, but the Romans taking over the most civilised Greek culture and religion. Of course it is not all bad news for if there are ideas that are recognised as being of real worth then the new worship and understanding may be able to embrace them to the good of the new, incorporating the best of both! (Perhaps not!!!) Hence 'Harvest Festival' and the like.

However, if all of that is not working then the last trick is to call the old religion evil. Not only was it not strong enough to defend the old nation, not only are the practices old- fashioned and slightly askew, but in reality the old Gods had enslaved 'you', not letting you grow and stand up for what you really think and can do. They are EVIL and are to be shunned and fought against. Hence there was no Satanism until Christianity was established. Hence the image of the Devil is that of the Goat or Horned One, the Baal or Pan of earlier religions. Fear is a very effective weapon in the domination armoury, so in consequence, look at the most taboo of the present religion and you will probably find the most sacred of the previous older religion!

Take great care though, for I think it is a mistake to equate the New Age Movement with the Old Religion of either wing of Druidism or Wicca. We have no continuity of thought from those times and ideas for, as I said, the Celtic language was spoken rather than written. It is all very well simply to call them Pagan times and the New Age as Neo Pagan, but it is sheer speculation to equate the two. In fact there are obvious discrepancies, given a little thought.

It can be seen from the legends handed down of the Old Religion that there was a hierarchy of Priesthood, both within the male and the female aspects. There was authority and a consensus of opinion of what was considered 'orthodox' and acceptable, a consensus possibly stretching right across Europe from Ireland to the Caucasian Mountains and beyond. Certainly archaeological research suggests that there was cooperation between the various regions, and trade existed in artefacts and ideas that held the Neolithic peoples together. It was a 'High' religion. How different that is from today!

Today there is no coherent authority in the New Age Movement. A person can be a 'Master Practitioner' or an Arch-Priest or Priestess simply by claiming to be just that – and remember that empty vessels make the most noise. That is why I speak of it as a Movement and not a religion in its own right. It is more a collection of ideas with some kind of collective identity – hard to define – but it is still a mishmash of concepts borrowing heavily from as far afield as the Mediterranean myths and legends, the Shamanism of the Native American, the Theosophy and Spiritualism of Madame Blavatsky, Astrology, far eastern philosophies and meditation practices, as well as half-constructed or half-'remembered' lore from Pagan times.

Even so, this mishmash presents a very real challenge to religious thinking of today in the Northern Hemisphere, and one that the Church as a whole has tended to ignore. Whether that is because the Church does not see that the New Age movement presents any theological challenge or simply because it does not understand the nature of the New Age, who can guess, but I think the Church does itself no favours by its attitude of dismissal. I would go as far as to say, that it is very much because the Church of the last decades has been dismissive and more concerned with its own navel gazing that the New Age has grown as fast as it has!

The Church has spent so much effort and thought in whether the priesthood should include women, or debated the worth of Rite A, Rite B, the Alternative Prayer Book, gay priests, Sunday trading, 'happy clappy' services and the like, that it has lost its sense of vocation. It has been more caught up with internal debate and 'demythologising' the scriptures to the point that it has lost its sense of wonder and mystery that are core aspects of the spiritual life, so of course people have looked elsewhere for answers on spiritual matters.

It is very easy, therefore, for the Church in these lands to take the extra step and not only discard the almost forgotten remnants of the Christian Celtic ways but see them as embracing something of the Old Religion's emphasis on Nature and Mother Earth. They fall within the 'Take Over' thought process and are castigated in consequence. Indeed trying to unravel the various threads to see what is of value from the past, as well as not throwing away the good in the new, is a daunting task and it is a very brave person who stands up against the present church ways and says otherwise. Yet I understand that this is a task that every person who begins to mature in the spiritual way must undertake for themselves. God is bigger and better than any human can even begin to conceptualise. God is there to be revealed to everyone who seeks, albeit in their limited ability and way. I despair of the dogma and entrenched positions that people of all religions take, although I can understand that the challenge of new ideas may exacerbate their insecurity and become counterproductive to forward thinking. A person cannot face insecurity if they are feeling unsafe. However, we all need to address the spiritual poverty as best we know how or are able to make, and that means facing those challenges.

When was there advertised a Lent course on Angels, or Spiritual Beings, spiritual dimensions or even simply how to pray? When was the Church considered as an authority on Meditation or personal spiritual development and discipline? When did it have the guts to leave dogma and encourage individuals to explore the spiritual world all around them, being an authoritative guide in these matters? Why has it not seen the spiritual famine in society and spoken in ways that can be heard? What is the treasure that Christ presented that the Church's form of evangelism often seems to castrate? Is it because the Church itself is so spiritually poor that it cannot see beyond the navel gazing and declare itself spiritually bankrupt? It needs that proverbial stick of dynamite beneath its collective backside and start to realise its God-given purpose once again! Thank goodness Truth and God do not depend exclusively upon our efforts!

6

So is the present Church all bad?

Please, please note that there is the world of difference between Christianity and the Church. Where Christianity is a worldwide religion, the Church is a collective noun that includes many expressions of that religion. The Church, in its multitudinous form, endeavours to be the expression of Christianity. It encompasses the major institutional forms such as Roman Catholic, Greek and Russian Orthodox, Episcopalian, Lutheran, Protestant, Baptist, and so on and so on, but where orthodoxy makes way to heresy is a minefield of debate and I dread to venture there. For the moment let me consider 'the Church' as being more mainstream than being more an inclusive or overall 'Christian' expression.

In that case, the Church *has* had its successes in the past, but it has also made so many mistakes, especially when it has relied more on politics, power and wealth rather than on spirituality, morals and ethics. It has been found wanting, monstrously so on occasions, so the Church has been reformed several times in its history. A thousand years of monastic life was overturned in five during the English Tudor years! The Puritans, Quakers, Methodists, Baptists etc. have all had their time, with tremendous social change initiated by their groups such as the Clapham Sect. Yet that kind of reform has not been limited just to the more Protestant wing. The Oxford Movement was of the 'High' end of the churchmanship spectrum, re-establishing the sense of continuity from Apostolic times with its innate authority of Church Orders. But *now* the Western World is a multicultural world with many religions represented, and the Church – of whatever denomination or sect – is an irrelevance to most people, no matter how hard that is to hear by Church people, parishioners only seeking out the Vicar or parish church for family funerals, weddings or the occasional Midnight Mass. The *overall* membership of the Church is in decline, the membership is getting elderly, income and assets are dwindling as the burden of maintenance and revenue costs grows ever higher. It desperately needs to be reformed once again and I am sure that it will fade away altogether unless it regains its spiritual vocation.

Christianity, however, is just as popular, though not necessarily recognisable in any traditional form. There is a growing phenomenon throughout the hemisphere that Christ's words are 'claimed' by churches, house groups, sects, heresies, and even many New Age groups, despite the re-emergence and prominence of the Goddess. Many people are still desperately searching for spiritual food and they do recognise Christ as a past great teacher. But where is the Church's voice of authority on *spiritual* matters? Where is its interpretation of Christ's words for today? Where is its answer to the present day challenge? It needs to meet the New Age Challenge.

I only wish part of the Celtic Christian Church were still here today. It spoke the same language, metaphorically speaking, as the New Agers and spiritually seeking populace, yet it had such authority, unlike *both* the modern Church and the New Age movement as a whole. It was not so caught up with social reform, political power, celebrity status and wealth. It was so much more concerned with the quiet cycles of Nature, of the unseen effects of relationship within the environment, of 'sacredness' of Life and respect of gender and the complementing of male and female and of 'psychic stuff'. It offered a spiritual path and understanding that stretched back to the earliest times of the Church. In fact it was the early church of North Africa which evolved into the Celtic Church in Western Europe that had been the spiritual giant and 'thinker' of those early days. It is the echoes of the Celtic Church that resonate with today's issues and challenges, but that leadership and the past spiritual 'thinkers' are not present anymore. Shame!

Christianity has stood the test of time. Christianity has withstood schism from within and assault from without. It claims an academic integrity that is sadly lacking in the New Age. It cannot be contained by any church denomination. It has changed its outward form many times over the centuries. That outward form is fundamentally changing today as its present 'incarnation' dies. Yet Christianity is freely available for any genuine seeker of spiritual truth to embrace. Christ came to show spiritual truth to anyone.

7

For Goodness Sake Pray Attention there!

So at least from a Christian perspective, why write about prayer? Answer – Because I see prayer as being at the heart of spirituality.

Letter writing is a dying art. I remember being taught in Junior School how to write a letter but I don't suppose they do that anymore. There was a right way and a wrong way to write one, and you invariably began it with "Dear Sir or Madam", being very polite, but you took your time to think through what you wanted to say, making several stabs at it until it seemed comfortable and succinct before sending in the post. Today you are more likely to be taught about emails, texting and how to Skype, and never mind your English or Grammar.

So, for example, if I were to write to Suzanne, my wife, after we had had an argument the previous evening, I might write in full righteous indignation along the lines of "Dear Mrs Littlewood. With regards to the exchange of the 15 inst, I respectfully point out...". But on second thoughts I would then screw the paper up into a small ball and throw it in the bin and start again. "Dear Suzanne. I know it was hard to hear my points last night but...". And after another screwing up of paper and another stab. "Dearest Suzanne. I am sorry...". Much better.

Some letters need to be quite formal and others more personal, but they are all thought out with (hopefully) plenty of time taken as the best means of getting a point across, of relating with the other person. And we always also end the letter in a prescribed manner. If we started with "Dear Sir" then we finish with "Yours faithfully". If it was "Dear Mr Smith" then it should finish with "Yours sincerely"; if "Dearest..." then it finishes with "With Love", and so on.

The vast majority of our relating to God is in the form of a letter, a celestial letter, even if it is not posted anywhere? So we begin, "Dear Heavenly Father" or "Dear Lord", and certainly there has been much thought gone into the corporate letters of public worship. There is no need to repeatedly screw up the paper to think things through for generations of worshipers have already been there and done that. We cannot improve on the letter but just follow on using the same format. Yet you can imagine God receiving that letter and groaning and thinking 'what that one, *again*'.

However, even if the prayer is more personal or extemporary then the usual format is still followed, so it begins in the same way and then usually goes on to tell God all about a situation (as if He doesn't know about it) and ask that He intervenes in a particular way according to how we think the situation should be resolved! What is the joke? 'If you want to make God laugh tell Him your plans for the future'.

But no matter what kind of celestial letter it is there is usually also the prescribed form of ending it as well, namely "Through Jesus Christ our Lord. Amen". And that word 'Amen' is so, so important, for that tells God that we have finished praying!!!! He can stop listening then and our thoughts revert to being private!! If that isn't another facetious thought!

Just as an aside, the word 'Amen' is an Old Greek word that translates simply as 'Truly'. It is just an emphasis – that's all, not a 'signing off' or anything like it.

So going back to letters, of course it would be a very strange kind of relationship that Suzanne and I would have if we only passed each other letters, formal or otherwise. We communicate in all manner of ways such as by touch, gesture, gifts, and of course the spontaneous spoken words. Even so, communication can be fraught. So, for example in non-verbal communication, I might want to say that I love Suzanne so I buy her some choco-lates or, remembering the advert 'to say it with flowers', a bunch of roses or the like. I would be saying ' I love you' but it is likely that she will immediately think 'now what have you done wrong?'. It might not be like that in prayer, but just as in our earthly personal communicating with one another, so we can use non-verbal ways of communicating with God. We might light a candle with a particular person in mind as a form of intercession, or sprinkle water as a blessing, or re-enact that most profound sacrament of using bread and wine in Holy Communion. We don't have to send that celestial letter to pray.

Yet even the words themselves may be ambiguous and have more than one meaning as we say them. So for example choosing a very mundane situation of a speaker prompting people to vote for him after a corruption scandal in a local political ward, I might say, "Vote for me, John Littlewood [earnestly spoken]. These shenanigans need looking into [equally earnestly spoken]. So vote for me – you know it makes sense [spoken with emphasis]". Or I could say, "Vote for me, John Littlewood [spoken quietly with a knowing smile]. These shenanigans need looking into [spoken with a querying modulation]. So vote for me – you know it makes sense [spoken with a tap to the nose]". So although exactly the same words are spoken, the first time the speaker is out to right a wrong but the second speaker is suggesting he will follow the line of corruption again and 'you scratch my back and I will scratch yours'.

No matter what form of communication we use to relate with one another, it is the intent behind the words, letter or gestures etc. that we are endeavouring to convey and not the words or gestures themselves. So it is concerning prayer, if we think it is the words themselves that do the business of communicating, even if it is the words of the Lord's Prayer, then we are no better off than braying to the Moon for there is nothing magical about those words. It is no good just prattling off a sequence of well-worn words. It is what is behind the words, symbols or gestures that is important. It is the intent behind them that is the actual praying. And the good news – and bad news – is that that is precisely what can happen in prayer, for God knows the secrets of our hearts. And what an awesome thing that truly is.

Do you remember the 'God Spot' on the 'wireless' – for it was not called radio in those days – on the 'Light Programme' or 'Home Service', called 'Lift up your hearts'? That is the phrase that is used before the Prayer of Consecration in the Communion Service, and it depicts exactly what I mean. We offer our hearts and minds to God as we endeavour to relate to Him in some way. That is what prayer is all about. We meet God at a deep inner place as we externalise our intent, be it corporately or privately. We commune with God. Then we are in Communion.

So be very careful, for if we pray by rote without due thought then we are conveying disinterest! If we recite a prayer but our minds are elsewhere then that is our prayer! On the other hand though, if we truly care for someone as we pray then that is true intercession; if we are truly grateful then that is a true prayer of thanksgiving; if our hearts are full then that is true Communion; if we have a relationship with God then we must put time and thought and our hearts into relating. That is Prayer.

Amen!

So can anyone of any religion pray? And does it have to be a 'Christian' celestial letter?

I sometimes want to cry when I hear, 'No one comes to the Father except by me' (St John's Gospel chapter 14 verse 6), when it is bandied about as a 'proof text' that Christianity is the only religion that God endorses, for in that verse Jesus is reported as saying that He is the Way, the Truth and the Life, and no one comes to the Father except by Him. So there!!!! See!!!

What a most arrogant load of elitist utter claptrap!

No, No, No, No, No. It does *not* mean that everyone has to become a Christian in order to be at one with God. It simply means that Christ enabled anyone or everyone to approach God if they seek to do so. This is the *only* place in the whole of the New Testament that such an elitist idea can be construed 'explicitly', and even St Paul doesn't go that far! St John's Gospel is all about *in*clusion not *ex*clusion.

John sees far beyond the physical event of the Crucifixion to something of awe inspiring spiritual significance. Hence the major use of symbols in the writings for words are insufficient to describe this. John is the bridge builder and tries to bridge the gaps between differing theological and religious persuasions of his day, between Jew and Greek, between God's Elect (the Jewish chosen ones) and the Gnostic philosophies. And he does this by using the special theological word 'Logos – *Word*'.

- The 'Word' was God but the 'Word' became flesh (John 1v14).
- The 'Word' was also the Creator (John 1v3).
- The 'Word' was the Light of *all* men (John 1v5). (Author's italics)

John's message is one of *inclusion* and not exclusion, and the biggest bridge of all to be made is between God and mankind and that is possible through Jesus. The Crucifixion is the great reconciling event of all time. It is the greatest work of all, for when Christ dies reconciliation is accomplished. So that verse, *in the context of John's Gospel – where it belongs –* is saying that the spiritual event of Christ's Death has made it possible for everyone to be at one with God, no matter what religious route they might attempt.

Anything else is the most arrogant nonsense and bigoted doctrine to condemn all other religions and spirituality as being worthless.

The underlying fundamental assumption that John makes is that Christ's mission was to make such inclusion possible, and this was done by the Crucifixion. It was this single act by Christ that was of Cosmic significance – hence about half of his gospel is about the event, with the Resurrection tacked on almost as an afterthought. "It is finished. It is done," are the reported words spoken by Jesus as he dies. It is not something others even have to understand and accept – it is simply done. And we read that the curtain of separation between the people and the 'Holy of Holies' in the Jewish Temple at Jerusalem was torn in two from top to bottom at that moment.

So can anyone of any religion pray? The answer must be, 'of course' – "through (because of) Jesus Christ our Lord! Amen".

8

So where do we go from here?

Of course, being a Christian priest I need to take into my jottings doctrines of Salvation and Redemption, but as they are such heavyweight theological terms I shall leave them to one side for the moment until I have commented upon concepts of spirituality in more everyday or all encompassing terms.

When describing humankind there are some things that are universal, some ethnic, some of the clan or family, some to do with gender and some unique to each individual respectively. At the moment I am interested in the universal, for I go along with St John and believe that Christ's Crucifixion was effective for all.

Furthermore, usually such describing of humankind is categorised into physical, mental and spiritual aspects, but the very word 'spiritual' raises religious concerns, and I am at pains at this juncture not to fall into the trap of referring to religions and religious thought forms. To that end I prefer to talk about spirituality as part of the higher functions of the mind using such terms as Judgement, Integrity, Wisdom, Honour, Compassion and Sacredness, and, as I see it, these are universal aspects of humanity.

Everyone has both masculine and feminine attributes be they male or female. Masculinity has connotations of 'doing' whilst femininity has connotations of 'being'. This is nothing to do with gender, sex or sexuality – gay or straight. It is about aspects within a person that are seen to be associated with either male or female but belong to neither gender. So first let me consider some aspects of the higher mind associated with masculinity – the God within.

Possibly the most profound and debatable point I make is that I do not see Integrity as an attribute that is earned. Moral and ethical codes are things of the conscious mind, and can be developed and worked upon consciously. Through conscious understanding, conscience can be 'pricked', but that still remains a conscious process. I am looking below the conscious, within the subconscious or deep mind. This is the home of guilt and remorse, and integrity is allied and very present. Guilt may be felt because of moral codes instilled and programmed through conscious effort, but it is integrity that promises to do something about it, and therefore integrity can be considered a masculine attribute. Integrity may be moribund. It may need coercion and cajoling through guilt, but I believe it is present in every human being somehow. It is a universal aspect of being human. In that sense, it is given by God by virtue of that individual being alive even though it may just need to be acknowledged and freed to act. In that sense Integrity, Honour and Wisdom are allied and tend to be considered as part of a person's masculinity.

One could therefore say that the measure of spirituality must include the *intensity, strength or depth* of integrity – or the lack of it(!) – of that individual, and is not something dependent upon doctrine or dogma but some inner urging to make a stand or 'do' something about a situation.

In 'church speak' this is another way of talking about the doctrine of 'Original Righteousness' as compared with 'Original Sin'. Both doctrines are part of the church's belief system but hardly anyone has heard of Original Righteousness although nearly everyone has heard of Original Sin! They are opposite sides of the same coin.

Similarly Sacredness or Holiness is allied to Compassion and the Utmost Respect to all forms of life and relationship, and so ascribed to a person's femininity – or the Goddess within. The state of Holiness is not earned. It cannot be won through conscious effort but it is something that is found or revealed to be present within. It is also given by God by virtue of the person simply being alive, life being the gift from God, so it is not a 'gift' in the sense of Christian Gifts of the Spirit. Rather it is that it needs just to be embraced and delighted in. I see it as something that develops and grows, like *'fruit* of the spirit' – and in that sense of growth there is a *degree* of holiness. The *state* of holiness is something revealed, surrendered to and accepted – a state of 'being', not 'doing', and thus feminine.

So one therefore also needs to say that the measure of spirituality must include the depth or degree of Holiness or Sacredness, and is also therefore not something dependent upon doctrine or dogma of religion, although it could be talked about as such within the previously mentioned doctrine of Original Righteousness.

Referring to my third Essay, therefore, I have no doubts in accepting other forms of spirituality expressed through various religions and religious practices for we are all part of the human race and we all have such attributes of the God within and the Goddess within – or as St John puts it – the Light that lighteth every man. The light may be dim in some people, but it is still present to some degree. This is a universal given, so no one religion has the monopoly on spirituality.

But I *am* a Christian and I do believe that Jesus Christ is part of God, and so for me I see Christian spirituality as being a measure of being Christ-like. However, I will unpack that a bit later on.

9

The Sanctity of All Life

Despite the collective wisdom of all the religions throughout the ages, there is trouble in talking about spiritual things. It was easier when thinking about spirituality in the last essay in that at least I could use allied terms such as Integrity, Wisdom, Sacredness or Holiness, but to focus on the unseen – if that is not almost a contradiction in terms – is far harder. What is the essence of spiritual or being spiritual or a spiritual being?

To attempt an answer let me state that I believe we are part of Gaia and not just a part of Mother Nature.

That might sound a strange beginning but it states the principle that I believe is extant and shows, for us, the significance or importance of the complexity of the total environment and ecology systems. Let me start with the very physical world around us.

Mother Nature can be likened to a collection of creatures that live in a symbiotic relationship with their environment. In other words there is a food chain that starts with a lowly form of vegetation, a small animal feeds on this, then predators live upon each other in increasing size or ferocity, discharging waste along the way, until the 'top dog' rules, dies, rots so that the vegetation can thrive on the resulting matter. It is said that nature does not like a vacuum so an evolving niche of apparent safety, such as nettles in the vegetable kingdom or jellyfish in the animal kingdom, is soon found to be a ready source of food by a further evolving predator higher up the food chain, and evolution continues the process of making new species of plant and creature, even though this may take many thousands of years. It sounds mechanical, but there is an observable truth of "Nature is bloody in tooth and claw" and the 'top dog' is Mankind who often ignores the consequences of his actions upon the rest of Creation. That continues until part of the food chain breaks down due to over feeding or there is a change in the climate, and then a new order must appear.

Gaia, on the other hand, is more like a single organism. There are numerous cells to that organism and the organism might be continually changing its appearance as some cells grow or decline, new cells come into being and old cells die out, but the essential life of that organism continues. The whole of planet Earth's biosphere can be thought of as that single organism, and although a simple organism as depicted by Professor James Lovelock's *Daisyworld* may be able to live as planet Earth, he shows that a much more complex organism is more likely to be stable and thrive as a self-regulating, limiting yet evolving life form. In such a situation there cannot be considered any one cell more important than any other and diversity is the means towards stability, for that is 'not putting all one's eggs in one basket'. That being the case, the greater the diversity of cell life the more stable the organism becomes. The reverse is also true in that extinction of diverse cells leads to the decline or ill health of the whole organism and, if not checked, its eventual suicide!

That sounds rather 'airy fairy' or New Age Philosophical, but in real life on the very local level it has bite! This works out that we need to respect the different parts of the total environment, not only that of the human realm but also of the mineral, plant, bird, animal and even the unseen realms, and to acknowledge the most complex relationships that exist between them all. We should further recognise that as this complexity gives stability to the whole, so we should try not to exploit nor be exploited by any single group or part of it, especially human. We need all aspects of our world for a wholesome, healthy Life, and that whole to keep a balance between the dynamic and sometimes conflicting tensions of the individual parts.

In other words, it is not a case of "It would be nice to have some animals" or "Let's have a stab at Self-Sufficiency", but to deliberately increase the diversity of flora and fauna within our sphere of influence in the world – if at all possible. The place and circumstances will set limits on the type and number of animals and plants, but the Gaia concept demands we do our bit to help and try to be aware of the possibilities. That is being part of Nature's Green Machine rather than being apart from it. But it also means that as each new variety of plant or species of animal or creature make their appearance, then the relationships between them all increase in complexity. Some of those relationships fall into the subtle signal category, but these can still be experienced by sensitive souls as a greater feeling of harmony and dynamism all around us, of which we are a part. Occasionally the perception is acute and spoken of in terms of actual sight, sound or sensation, and this is the basis of super-normal or supernatural phenomena. However, the subtle signal, which is the basis of psychic sensitivity, is the 'nuts and bolts' of religious, spiritual or magical experience. It grows out of a consequence of respect, awareness and experience of the connectedness of all life, and so spirituality of all kinds is therefore a factor of that connectedness.

Respect for Gaia is not just a 'nice' idea but a real experience that involves people in ways that most have little understanding of. That does not lessen the interaction, however, it only means that the participants have little appreciation of what is going on and of the consequences for both positive and negative effect.

However, it is necessary to point out that *everything affects everything else*, and so it is impossible to just be an observer of life all around us and not be involved. We cannot help but interact in some way with everything and at many different levels of being.

So back to those unseen realms, and I think it best if I try to define my terms.

I see 'being spiritual' as another way of talking about spirituality, but with an implicit degree of recognised holiness associated about that person. Unfortunately it also seems to have connotations of acting in a religious fashion, so it engenders a certain amount of confusion in the general use of the term. It is *not* about religiosity but the inner qualities of degree or intensity of integrity, wisdom, compassion, respect and holiness or sacredness.

A spiritual being, on the other hand, would constitute a non-physical living entity or a citizen of the unseen realms. There is normally an understanding of intrinsic spirituality associated with such a being, but that is not always and necessarily the case. This being might impinge upon the physical in some way, having areas of influence to directly bring about change, or it might have an ability to inspire or frighten other creatures or beings, even of the physical world, through various means of communication. Such a being has traditionally been called an angel, demon, Deva, Manu, God or Goddess, ghost, wraith, or spirit, and so on.

A spiritual force would constitute a non-physical influence upon the physical or mental areas of life that is directed in some way by another being, and not necessarily by a spiritual being. Such force has traditionally been thought of as prayer, healing, blessing, cursing or ill wishing, magic or the like.

The ability to manipulate a spiritual force, either consciously or unconsciously, would therefore be inextricably linked in some way to spirituality, by its application, intensity, wholesomeness, goodness (or otherwise) and outcome. Such manipulation would not be the prerogative of any single religion, ethic or philosophy, but common to all to some degree or other. Furthermore, I understand that there are universal rules or laws that govern such spiritual forces in just the same way that physics define the laws of Nature. It is not that physics, science or religion make up the laws but rather these are naturally occurring phenomena that are discovered and rationalised in their respective ways.

The most easily understood spiritual law is that 'we reap what we sow'. So if respect for other aspects of Gaia is upheld then respect will ultimately be given in return. If we respect others and other kinds of being then we retain self-respect. Indeed to take this much further – if we love ourselves then we must have love for others, and that includes love for God as well. And haven't you come across that before somewhere??!!

In this way there is a direct relation between honour, compassion and all of the higher functions of the mind; a direct relation to spirituality or spiritual growth that boils down to upholding the sacredness or sanctity of life.

I have been told this is another way of talking about "mindfulness", which is perhaps a Buddhist buzz word being brought into daily use, but it seems to ring true, and who was more mindful than Jesus; mindful of his surroundings, mindful of himself, mindful of others and of God. Being aware of one and respectful of one makes us closer to another and the connection relationship keeps growing out like a tree deepening its roots into the ground and extending its branches to the light.

That, in my view, is an inescapable cause and effect that is a backdrop to Life that works itself out in some most mysterious way, explained by the various religions in different scenarios of reward or punishment in accord with their respective dogma.

10

So is there any advantage in being a Christian?

Obviously as a Christian priest I must say – yes, of course!!!

However, Christianity is not a tidy 'once upon a time' thought out religion. It might have made matters so much easier if it had been, but unfortunately it has evolved in a most tortuous fashion and is thus known as a revealed religion. What I mean is that initially, and subsequently from time to time, an individual had some kind of mysterious or 'religious' experience that had to be thought through to bring some kind of understanding and inter-pretation. As these experiences were shared and talked about so subsequent experiences had to be accommodated within a growing body of knowledge that grew into an accepted 'lore' or history, but one which could be adapted over time. In this way a recognised orthodoxy was gradually established which contained accepted doctrine for this or that area of life that continuing experiences had to be compared with. At the same time an accepted corporate authority or knowledgeable group of elders grew alongside the growing body of lore that had both a positive aspect of curbing the more extreme views that might have been expressed from time to time, yet producing a negative aspect or mighty inertia to progressive thinking.

Past events and the historical evidence would have been looked at a fresh from time to time to bolster shaky foundations to specific ideas or provide 'evidence' to the current way of thinking. History would have taken on new aspects of under-standing as new theories were presented to explain why something or other happened in a particular way. The hand of God would have been sought within that explanation and a changing way of looking at God slowly evolved. The histories, which in time became venerated and known as sacred 'scrip-tures', would have had to be challenged, adapted, rewritten or even duplicated from a different perspective and presented alongside the older existing story. So a 'canon' or accepted writings became established alongside the authority of the religious leaders.

On top of that, of course there was the political interplay between differing factions within the body of believers, even from the initial stages of the evolving religion. It was never simply a matter of trying to understand the experiences and come to an understanding of whom and what God was, but also the very human matter of power politics and standing in the community that had to be a factor. Academic and intellectual integrity, as well as spirituality, might be considered as second best to the more immediate satisfaction of gaining respect from one's peers and power over lesser mortals. Such is the fallout of any group or society. So why should a religion be any different.

Then there would have been the sudden 'lurches' of religious growth when momentous happenings could not be contained within the orthodoxy of the day. New factions would have emerged, or if the emerging theology was too radical, then a sect or even breakaway group would have formed. Even new religions could be born, with their roots and sacred body of lore already provided for. It didn't mean that every new religion had to be formed from scratch. So, for example, Christianity grew from Judaism and subsequent schisms produced Orthodoxy, Protestantism, Celtic Christianity and so on. And all the time the theology of the day would take a battering as twists and turns of societal interplay brought greater revelation of God and God's world around us.

And behind all of this individuals had to see how their own spiritual walk took on meaning from the events in their lives, how they came to terms with suffering and unfulfilled dreams and vision, and as to what the meaning of life was truly all about.

That is why doctrine changed as the 'revealed' interpretation became redundant, for society never stays still but moves forward, and thinking has to change with the times. Unfortunately it also usually meant that doctrine was always behind the times for it is only after much discussion that a new orthodoxy is established. Time and tide wait for no man.

Take, for example, those heavyweight doctrines of Salvation and Atonement.

It is absurd to think that those doctrines were initially considered and formed by simply sitting down and thinking about it! They were not concepts that would have been embraced or the words even come to mind. The beginnings of the Christian doctrine of Salvation, in fact, came about within another religious framework about 3,000 years ago. It wouldn't even have been thought of as a religion at that time but more of a family religious quirk, and only through the family gathered around a totem or family shrine talking of a spiritual being that seemed to be looking over them, protecting and guiding them as they wandered through a harsh landscape. In this case they named the guiding spirit Yahweh and no doubt spoke of this being to comfort and strengthen each member so there was a sense of belonging to the family and standing together against the vagaries of neighbours and the struggle for survival. It was an 'Us and Them' mindset, and we need to stick together against Them. Particular stories would have been memorised and passed on to succeeding generations around the fire as teaching points to that family. Traditions would have been established and, if the family prospered, the family numbers would have grown along with their family sense of identity, looking back to their founders or patriarchs with great respect. To belong meant to be safe for there was safety in numbers, and the only way for new members to be included was by marriage or by special adoptive decree. To be born into the family meant you didn't have to say anything, any jingle to be included and safe. You just were part of the family.

Such a family was descended from Abraham, Isaac and Jacob.

Of course as the Israelite family grew so did the concept of the protecting guiding spirit. No longer was it proved to be just a small family 'familiar' but a presence that grew in stature as challenges were met and the family grew in wealth and respect. Such a powerful spirit seemed to give exclusive attention to the family's well-being over the surrounding peoples and land that the clan travelled through. However, the clan took a giant leap forward in both numbers and influence when Joseph, the man of the many coloured coat, ended up living in Egypt, and Yahweh was known as the God of the Israelites.

However, the two greatest leaps forward for both the familial identity and the family's emerging religion were the two migrations, those of leaving Egypt and later leaving Babylon. The first exodus was lead by Moses where the 'family' that had first moved to Egypt, left as a 'nation' after momentous happenings there and as they journeyed to the Promised Land via the receiving of the Covenant or Ten Commandments from Yahweh, from God. The second exodus was led by religious leaders or prophets, where after a forced exile of the prominent citizens by a conquering army to the land of Babylon, they went as a nation but exited as a 'Holy People'.

By this time the sense of belonging to a single family had taken on the proportions of being an elite; God's special chosen people. And this full-blown doctrine of God's Elect would hold sway as part and parcel of being an Israelite or Jew, held until the time of Christ when Jesus brought revolutionary ideas to the moribund traditions and spirituality of the established Covenant or Testament.

Even after Christ's death and resurrection the new sect within Judaism tended to be only for Hebrew Christians. It wasn't until people like St Peter, and especially St Paul, rattled the orthodoxy of the day by proclaiming that the gentiles could also be grafted into the noble root of the family by Baptism and Faith that included both an act of stepping forward for Baptism and a statement of belief. So, the doctrine changed in emphasis from that of genetic family membership to one of being safe within the fold of Christ – that of Salvation, of belonging by faith as members of the new family of God – The Church.

Soon after the events of the gospel stories the doctrine of Salvation was explained in considerable detail by the writer of the Epistle to Hebrews. The Church, which had by then separated from Judaism and established its own leadership, accepted the Epistle as an orthodox book of the new canon, which was called the New Testament. I am sure it made excellent sense to those early Hebrew Christians, but even in those days the Jewish concept of Temple sacrifice, Paschal Lambs, Sacrifice of Atonement, orders of priesthood according to Melchizedek and the like would have been difficult for non-Jews to understand. We, in our day and age, haven't a snowball's chance in Hell of understanding all the nuances and implications. From then on the circumstances of the day demanded a re-examination of the doctrine as the society in which the Christian religion was being preached changed out of all recognition to its original setting.

'The blood of the martyrs was the seed of the Church' is a saying that explains the next great challenge of the new religion. Martyrdom of Christians at the hands of the Romans is a well-documented historical fact, and rather than being safe and protected as a church family member it was decidedly unsafe to be known as a follower of Christ. The emphasis within the doctrine of Salvation moved to that of Atonement, to include identification with Jesus in his own martyrdom on the Cross. Salvation no longer meant being physically safe or secure but as the eventual reward of being with Christ in the heavenly realms. However, it also meant that strength could be realised to face the persecution and probable martyrdom by the power of God or the Holy Spirit in that identification with Christ. That is what

Atonement or At-one-ment evolved into that had relevance for those suffering people. It was a doctrine that had bite in those times. It had an experiential outcome. It helped those who embraced the Faith. It was a living faith and religion and not just a philosophical nicety. But let's move on.

After Christianity became the Established religion of the Empire and the world moved on into the Dark Ages, the emphasis also moved yet again. There was no need for martyrdom of the average disciple any more, for to be civilised meant you were automatically a Christian. The Western World was no longer pagan but basked in the universally accepted religion of Christ. Of course there were degrees of embracing it in that there were monastic orders and vocational vows, but the ordinary person had no other thought of belonging to any other religion for there was no other religion. Salvation had no relevance to everyday living for you were a Christian from birth – full stop. Salvation as an abstract idea was only relevant to the next life, although your immortal soul had to be protected through this one as it faced the superstitions and evils of devil worship and witchcraft that plagued the Dark Ages until the Renaissance and Reformation. Atonement during this dark time was the means to find faith to withstand temptation and evil influence as Christ's death showed that even the worst that the Devil could send against Jesus was insufficient to hold him. Christ triumphed over death even, so those who were followers of Christ could likewise triumph over the fiery darts of the evil one.

The overturn of the supreme or absolute power of the priesthood and the schisms that resulted from Martin Luther's declaration of Protest that heralded the Reformation brought in the classic doctrine of Salvation as proclaimed by the Evangelical. There had to be a personal change of heart to be born again as a son or daughter of God. Here is the birth of the Evangelical 'jingle' of 'being saved' or 'washed in the blood of Christ'. It was not simply a matter of going to church and following the religious practices and dictates of the priest. There had to be a step of faith of 'turning to Christ' and 'seeing the Light' like St Paul. Nothing else was sufficient to be sure of salvation from the fires of Hell. Christ's death was proclaimed as a 'Ransom for many' and so was the cost that God paid for the Redemption of individuals' souls. So St Paul's gospel or his letter to the Romans became the most important Epistle of the New Testament and only personal salvation by a public act of faith was acceptable for the Protestant at the time of the Reformation right through until the mid 1900s. Yet as a consequence this doctrine of Salvation meant that there was an 'us and them' situation that was just as separatist as that held by the earliest Jewish family as they travelled through hostile lands. No longer was there a sense of everyone being included in the family of the Church. The Church in England became the Church of England, with a Protestant and exclusive basis of faith.

Of course Christ the Redeemer was particularly relevant to a society that included a pawnbroker on every town's high street. Personal items were redeemed if they had been pawned and were valued. It was the credit system of the day for there was no plastic or buying on the 'never never' in those days. The doctrine was relevant to its times. However, times forever move on.

Today the 'hell fire and damnation' call to faith tends to draw embarrassment from those within earshot, with a certain amount of disdain and pity as a close second and third emotional response. The doctrine is so old fashioned and out of place that it speaks more about those using it as a proclamation of the gospel than those it is aimed towards. It takes the exclusive elitist ideas of the Jewish family and represents them as an exclusive dogma more in keeping with a sect or cult. That view of exclusivity I find repugnant.

However, it was mainly Roman Catholic theologians who reviewed the Atonement doctrines and came up with a novel and pertinent reworking. Since the early 1950s the question of authority has never been far away from the arena of theological discussion. "By whose authority do you speak?" "By whose authority do you make those promises?" By the authority of the Son of God, the authority of Christ.

The overhaul of the doctrine made use of the conclusion that the Resurrection was the event that put the seal on the authority of Jesus. No other event like it before the time of Christ or ever since has had such significance. Other people had apparently been revived from death as a physical body, or returned from the dead as a ghost or spirit, but no one had returned with both physical attributes and spiritual abilities. Jesus was unique. It was the Resurrected Christ that proved to those who saw him that the claims that had been made on his behalf were true. He was revealed as the Son of God. And if that was true then everything he had said, everything he had promised, everything he had done took on the significance of God. And he promised a spiritual rebirth through him.

What a long, long way from that campfire and the guiding, protecting spiritual presence. Yet that has been the development of the doctrine at the heart of the Christian gospel.

As far as I can see Jesus does not exclude anyone from 'belonging' or Salvation except by their own selfish or evil action or intent. 'We reap what we sow'. Those are his teachings. However, the advantage for the Christian is that Jesus handed on to his disciples teachings about all manner of spiritual things that had the authority of God. He is "the Door" or "Way" to go forward by taking to heart the essence of his teachings and opening one's eyes to the Truth of those spiritual laws, and to accept in faith that those promises hold true for each and every one of us. To embrace that idea is indeed like being born again to the things of the spirit.

That is not a denial of other Faiths and Religions or a betrayal to one's own, but to my mind it does hold a truly tremendous advantage or treasure for the follower of Christ.

11

So is there any advantage in being part of a Church?

On the one hand a church attendee would have the advantages of belonging to a group of like-minded people, but on the other hand would have the disadvantages of being constrained by them.

There is nothing so stirring to the soul as when a group of like-minded people sing the praises of God or join in fervent prayer or communion. It can be extremely uplifting. Worship is giving worth to God and to do so in such company gives so much extra meaning and significance to the act. In addition, the support of friendship, fellowship and other points of view cannot be under-estimated. It broadens the outlook on problems and issues. It helps the adherent through the lean or troubled times. The sense of belonging gives a sense of self-worth and self-respect as others find worth and respect for the adherent. Above all there is hopefully the guidance of trained and wise leaders whose vocation is to be a shepherd of Christ's flock and whose vocation has been recognised by the hierarchy of the establishment. It could be such a positive step to take to become an adult member of a worshipping community.

Unfortunately it can also have pitfalls and a negative influence. If the leadership is poor or non-existent then it is a matter of the blind leading the blind. Not only would the adherent not grow in spirituality but there is the very real disadvantage of falling into the trap of religiosity. Alpha courses have been introduced as a means of helping people make a step of faith, but as church numbers dwindle and pressure is applied to have bums on seats, then there is the beginnings of a cult attitude that is the very opposite of spiritual freedom and growth. Peer pressure is subtle to begin with and insidious in effect. The church member can become trapped in emotional and even financial commitments. The belonging can become a burden rather than a joy or simply a religious status paraded each Sunday to the loyal few gathering rather than a serving spiritual one.

Added to that there is the distinct possibility that the church members will be caught in the old evangelical trap of jingle calling, even though they may not be evangelicals. The mindset is such an insidious trap in that unless you say the magic words then you do not truly belong. You have to say, and even supposedly think, the same as everyone else! Jesus was quick to point out that Samaritans and even the gentile Roman Centurion were more spiritually mature than his Jewish audience at that time. To my mind that exclusivity shows more of the members' insecurity rather than your own, but the pressure can be enormous to comply. For their sake you have to conform! So as I wrote in my first essay, quality of leadership is so very, very important and the need is for mature teachers and teaching at the parochial level.

It is with a very heavy heart that I realise the quality of leadership is deteriorating rapidly, although the Church of England will take a few more years to shrink into historical obscurity. It doesn't matter if a person wants a 'happy clappy' get-together or to lose him or herself in the profound depths of Stainer's Crucifixion or Handel's Messiah, the matter of choice of worship must always remain with the person, and their satis-faction or sense of Communion or Fellowship is a personal thing. What does matter is if a person is truly seeking spiritual food but only receiving pap, for although there might remain a sense of something missing, comparison with real spiritual food will never take place.

It *should* be an advantage in belonging to a worshipping community, but on the whole I now believe it to be a veritable trap or cul-de-sac to the seeker after truth. It will take a wise and cautious person to avoid the pitfalls of belonging and still gain the comfort and support of fellow believers. It will take an even wiser person to realise the spiritual paucity of the Church and take steps to remedy the situation by taking that responsibility of the spiritual search upon him or herself whilst keeping the fellowship of corporate worship.

It is possible, but very lonely.

12

For Heaven's Sake – Where the heck are we Going?

The church in England, and in particular the Church of England, is irrelevant to the vast majority of the populace in the country. Interaction is more than likely limited to only Remembrance Sunday, Christmas (if that), most funerals and some weddings.

The Church has failed the people it is supposed to serve in that it no longer seems to have a relevant message to proclaim to the nation for today's societal issues, it seems to have no authority that people look to, it lacks spirituality and a spiritual message, preferring to navel gaze, give mixed messages about sexuality, paedophilia, integrity and ethics, or indulge in political or social debate. It has lost its way and is financially and, to a large extent, spiritually bankrupt. It is dying. Not to put too fine a point on it, to an observer standing outside the institution of the Church the hierarchy have failed the general body by their lack of insight and vision for the future, relying on a past heritage and inertial tradition. There has to be a most drastic reappraisal and change of policy if the tide is to be turned and if Christ's message is to be heard through the C of E.

On the other hand there is growth within the more radical religions and there continues to be a search for spiritual truth amongst the people as witnessed to by the rise in New Age philosophy and practice. People look beyond the confines of the bureaucratic and institutional body of the C of E to nature, psychic phenomena and alternative approaches to spiritual and religious thinking.

There is nothing sacred about the Church – although to some that might sound a bit blasphemous. However, the outer expression of the Christian faith is so very different in different parts of the world and has changed dramatically in the past in this country. At the time of the Dissolution of the Monasteries a one-thousand-year tradition was overturned in about 5 years. The domination of the monastic way of life gave way to the cathedrals and parish churches with their respective attendants, so there was nothing sacred in the Christian expression then but rather in the message of Christ given through the Church. So it is today. The form of the Church is changing whether we like it or not, and I believe God is big enough and wise enough to halt this or hasten it according to his will.

And so we come full circle in my musings, for generally the leadership is not present in the Church of England at the local level as the butter is being spread ever more thinly. The money is not there to pay the stipends of trained full-time clergy working in the parishes at grassroots level. Yet it is at this level the whole ministry of the Church is supposed to be focused. It is at this level of person to person that the gospel message counts. It is at this level that personal commitment begins. It is at this level that vocation is discovered in the membership. It is at this level that donations are regularly given. It is at this level that the main fundraising takes place. It is here that the diocesan level ultimately relies upon! But what happens? Parishes are being denied the necessary trained leadership and pastoral care of a fully committed priest.

I look around me and see people searching for authority on spiritual matters. I see the Church afraid to speak on spiritual matters!! The Church should be *the* authority on spiritual matters in these lands. This is absurd!

The best way of teaching is by example, but I wonder how many priests actually are able to teach on spiritual matters (!), for when visiting churches in this area I have to bite my tongue again and again at the paucity of sermon content and the lack of dignity, authority and spiritual presence that the celebrant proffers. Instead of Alpha courses and jingoism perhaps it is time to teach the basics of how to pray or how to meditate. When has there been a regular course on the various different kinds of healing gifts? What about teaching about the heavenly realms or Life after Death or spiritual beings or subtle energies or dreams or prophecy or second sight or psychic sensitivity or the relationship between magic, prayer and spirituality? These are the subjects that the New Age festivals cover and such festivals are *very* well attended. People want to know about this kind of thing and there are so many charlatans pouring forth upon these subjects and the content swallowed hook line and sinker. The country has lost its 'soul' with the consequence of lack of respect affecting all areas of life, and it is not going to regain it by listening to such twaddle. Indeed the media reports that the Church seems to be continually covering up unethical practice and inappropriate sexual liaisons, lost in its time bubble of liturgical theatre. No wonder the Church is rejected.

I would therefore like to make a few suggestions. The first is not to make the mistake of putting energies into bringing 'the young' to church attendance. Worship is not another name for Sunday School, for the outcome of such a policy is twofold. Firstly it is to lose the young adults when it is no longer 'cool' to attend church, for the Confirmation service is more likely to be seen as a passing out ceremony rather than an entry into adult commitment. And the other outcome is to lose the older generation of worshippers as they no longer find the worship meaningful in any way.

Worship is another way of saying 'worth-ship', so the weekend main service should be of worth to the worshipper as well as God being worshipped. It needs to sum up the challenges covered by the past week's problems or issues, both at a national or international level and at a personal or family level. It needs to prepare the individual to face the challenges of the following week. It needs to place the worshipper outside of all challenges and give that person a sense of worth in God's eyes and awe and love of God in the worshipper's eyes. It needs to be *relevant*. Sunday School – if it is any good – may succeed to some degree in doing that for primary school aged children. However, it cannot do that for adults if it is pitched for children. The main service of worship needs to be relevant to adults, so if any age group is to be targeted then somehow the young family group should be in the leader's sights. Once a parent (usually a mother) begins to attend by first being involved in a 'toddlers' group or young mums group, then youngsters will usually come along as a consequence. If the father can be enticed by meaningful, relevant teaching and a worthwhile adult experience, then the whole family will undoubtedly attend. There is the continuing worshipping community.

Another suggestion is to stop pussy footing around the issue of gender. No matter how much the politically correct people deplore the fact, men and women are not equal and cannot simply swap roles at the drop of a hat. As virtually all psychologists and counsellors will point out, men and women are not only physically different but basically think in different ways as well. The stereotypes exist because they portray a truism behind the images. That is the nature of stereotype. To be simplistic to the point of overstating things, men love by 'doing' and women love by 'being'. Generally speaking men show they care by putting up shelves and the like or working all hours of the day to bring in the cash. Women show they care by being with their partner and emotionally supporting their partner in whatever activity is being employed even if there is an inclination to the contrary. It isn't a thought-out course of action. It is an unconscious acceptance of how things are.

So although both men and women can be ordained and be called 'priest', their respective ministries should reflect the deeper inclination of that truism, and such be openly acclaimed. However, perhaps we can take a lesson from the Old Religion as far as ministry is concerned. They acknowledged the difference between the genders and, going with the flow, tended to polarise areas of influence. As I wrote before, if I have got it right, the history – the law (or lore and administration) and storytelling – were more the prerogative of the male priesthood, while healing, fecundity and intuition were more under the authority of the female priestesses or wise women. So for today in the Church of England, why not polarise ministry along the lines of stereotype. Of course both men and women can nurture suffering souls or administer a parish, but the Healing Ministry is more likely to resonate with the feminine and the Ministry of Word to resonate with the masculine. Let the Church acknowledge the differences and formalise the delineation and at the same time make better use of the respective inclinations, despite the PC attitude that is the hallmark of the thinking classes!

Above all the Church needs to be relevant to the issues of today, be an authority on spiritual matters and meet the challenge of the New Age philosophies. Mind, Body and Spirit festivals are big business and attract a huge interest by the general public. Health and Well-Being are very much to the fore about lifestyle and attitude, so why cannot the Church organise such an event? Why not have a financial stake in promoting such things and not be shy in having their own proclamation within it? Why cannot the Church provide courses within the Adult Education spectrum teaching Meditation, or give lectures on Angels, Spiritual Realms, compare Magic with Prayer and so on? Why leave it to the charlatans or self-claimed Masters? Let the Church stand up for itself, or is it afraid that it cannot compete?

One last suggestion at this stage (see later jottings) is that perhaps the policy of consolidating and rationalising that is so prevalent throughout the Church of England should not be taking place at the parish level at all but considered for the diocesan level instead. Neighbouring Dioceses could become amalgamated rather than have parishes merge into deanery-sized benefices, so saving high salaries as the non-productive administration roles are pared away. The resulting monies could be more usefully employed on the religious coalface, which would in turn be a form of investment in man power and resources.

But like most administrational top heavy institutions I cannot see the bosses taking such a policy to heart! At least one diocese has already been forced to become amalgamated with its neighbour, and on the news this week (November 2014) the Cornwall diocese is looking at a similar possibility, but being forced to that situation means it will be far, far too late to be effective. By that time the Church of England would be in its death throes.

I do not envy the diocesan hierarchy for if they have any nous about them they must see which way the wind is blowing and realise there is so very little they can do about it unless they are prepared to speak about the unspeakable to their neighbouring peers and get their cooperation before it is too late. But there is such a huge inertia to the institution that a lone voice has little chance of effecting a change, and such a step must appear as a betrayal to their calling. No doubt it would be met by a crusading protest of both clergy and laity, full of righteous indignation and zeal calling for resignations wholesale.

I wonder if that could be the trigger for renewal within the Church? Perhaps not!

Part II

Spirituality Reborn

13

What is So Sacred?

Let me play a mind game. Try to put yourself in the position of someone living in Neolithic times in the land that later became known as Great Britain. What kind of religion would have been prevalent or be the orthodoxy of the day?

I acknowledge that this is extremely speculative but even so we can have some idea as to how it might have been. The religion was matriarchal in nature. When survival depended upon fecundity of the land in all its aspects and guises then the female tended to be courted and revered over the male. It was the female who was the constant factor of life, the centre of the community who would have tended the fire and the young. The Sun may be thought of as male and the giver of Life, but in the same vein the Earth is undoubtedly female and holds the secret of birth and rebirth, bringing forth new life from within.

No doubt inheritance or the sense of belonging was passed through the female, for not being sexist but acknowledging the insinuation, even when ownership had predominance over community, surety of lineage could only be through the female. Lore might have been the provenance of either gender and Protection and War mainly the males' area of concern but Care, Healing and Fecundity undoubtedly laid within the females' sphere of influence.

It might seem strange to us in today's society but it wasn't until the last one-hundred years or so that the ordinary person in the street could divorce him or herself from any religious persuasion. The saying is that there are no atheists hiding in foxholes for when life is precarious then a certain amount of superstition or religious thinking comes to the fore. Any advantage is willingly sought, and before this last one-hundred years or so there could have been no conception of life without reference to the unseen, the mysterious or religion. So returning to the Neolithic times, then the female would have dominated the religious thinking and it would not have been a male divinity to be worshipped but a female one – a Goddess or Mother Earth.

What we know from the archaeological finds is that this religious form was extremely widespread and became the basis of the Celtic way of life from the westernmost part of Ireland to the Caucasian area of mid Russia. There was an accepted orthodoxy for the same art forms and religious expression was uniformly present. It was a 'high' religion and deeply ingrained in ordinary people. There were centres of religion and mighty constructions like Stonehenge and Avebury that would have taken tremendous resources and community effort to build and maintain. It was the cement that held together trade and commerce, civilisation and wealth. It was the overwhelming factor in life and survival – a matriarchal religion.

So, back to the thought experiment. Try to think what it would have been like when the orthodoxy was at its height. Can you imagine a person's surprise and refutation if it were proposed that the matriarchal religion would die and a patriarchal religion take over? Can you imagine how preposterous that would have been to their thinking? Do you not think that the more ardent followers would pledge their very lives to prevent such a happening? It would have appeared as blasphemy and sacrilege just to raise the possibility for, to them, they were talking about the most sacred aspects of their existence. Yet that switchover actually happened, not in an instant of course, but over many years. It was an extreme change. It was an utter and most profound change. It would have been the equivalent of a mega tonne explosion within religious thinking if it had happened overnight, but because it was spread over many years it crept up on the general populace and was hardly challenged at all. The most sacred was discarded for something new. Surely nothing like it could happen again.

But let's change the period of history and consider another revolution of a kind but within a particular religion and over a much shorter term.

Imagine the religious context in the Britain of Medieval times such as the years of the civil war between King Stephen and Empress Maud. The Christian religion was very well established by then and monasteries were a power in the land. These institutions were generally very wealthy, were large land owners and employers, and were the repository of medicine, history and general knowledge. They were the welfare system of their day. Their daily lives revolved around the monastic services. They were *the* expression of the Christian religion of the time in these lands. The ordinary folk would have been told what to believe and it would have been inconceivable for such people to think in any terms other than those given them.

Now imagine the religious context in the Britain of post-Tudor times. The Reformation had been and gone for the most part, leaving clearly delineated groups of people of various degrees of religious persuasion and expression. The whole spectrum could be found somewhere ranging from the Roman Catholic to the Puritan with the protestant Church of England holding the main central ground. The monasteries, in the main, were non-existent. The power of religion rested in Cathedrals and Bishops. The ordinary folk had to be careful in what they said for the religious thought police could descend upon them and imprison them for stating anything other than accepted orthodoxy, and indeed people had lost their lives for suggesting other under the accusation of witchcraft, heresy or treason. They were turbulent times when it was best to keep your head down or lose it!

What two very different expressions of Christianity. If someone in Medieval times had been told about religious life in the post-Tudor times was to be then I somehow think they would not have believed it could possibly happen. However, on this occasion the change did not take place over centuries but only over a single lifetime. In fact the actual physical expression of the dominance of monastic life was overturned in just 5 years when Henry the Eighth instigated the dissolution of the monasteries to bolster his failing treasury.

What seems so secure a way of thinking because of its sacredness and interwoven effect through all of life has been overturned more than once in these lands. The sacred is discovered to be not so sacred after all and the unchanging has changed dramatically. Excluding evangelistic zeal within a religious setting, Power, Might and Politics care little of God or religion unless it can be used to further their aims and objectives, as we can see from these changes.

People have touched the sacred with awe. People believe that nothing is more important than that sacred touch and have even gone the way of martyrdom because of their belief. People have believed that the expression of the sacred is so deep that it can never be surpassed. Unfortunately the most unpalatable truth that history teaches us is that God has had other ideas. If people believe they know the mind of God then God, of whatever gender(!), keeps changing His or Her mind!!

'Religious' people are committed people. They are people who truly believe they have been touched by God or know the Will of God. They are awed by the Sacred – as they understand that word. But looking back on history does raise that question as to what is sacred? Can the sacred be less than so and be open to re-evaluation?

I am sure you can think of similar scenarios of re-evaluation in today's world. I am sure that religious people who are not even fanatics in their chosen religion would not be able to countenance such a possibility for change – but as it has happened more than once in the past then I can see no reason why it cannot happen again in the future.

It is time to think the unthinkable and believe the unbelievable, but the unbelief of the unbelieving is unbelievable!

14

Astrological Red Herring?

It might seem a rather strange topic to embark upon but this is an interesting side issue in that astrological theory tells us that the world is moving through great ages that last approximately 2,000 years a piece.

You might recall that a few years ago there was a hit in the pop charts of a song from the musical 'Hair' called 'This is the dawning of the Age of Aquarius'. It was describing our time as the time of transition between one great astrological age to another, and in this case the moving was from the age of Pisces to the age of Aquarius. It is not as if the world wakes up one morning and has moved over, but rather the transition may take from 50 to even 150 years to complete, and during this time the world cannot be said to be in either age as the principles of either age might describe the characteristics of the society. In fact during the transition period life might be very complex and turbulent as the mix occurs and can be thought of as the new age's birth pangs.

The theory states that each great age has the characteristics associated with the astrological sign attributed to it. So the age that the world is moving out of should display Piscean traits to be gradually replaced by Aquarian traits.

Pisces is considered a spiritual sign at best or at least a religious sign of some order or degree. It is also interesting that the early Christian sign that the church adopted was the fish and Pisces is the sign of the fishes. However, that age would therefore be a time of religious activity and evangelistic zeal. Religions would rise and fall and religious power wax and wane as their respective spheres of influence changed with the tide of conviction and acceptance. Indeed the last 2,000 years of history that cover the Christian Era could very well be chronicled in terms of religion and religious expansion, both in the East as well as the West. Religion and religious power has dominated societies and peoples, with acts of imperialism often couched in religious terms and the implementation of the kingdom of God here on Earth. Of course the chronicles for that period could just as easily be couched in military, economic or political terms but let the astrological description stand for now.

The age that preceded the age of Pisces was the age of Aries and in this case the dominant traits would have been those of subjugation or assertion, and of course, of war. Naturally any histories of those times is bound to be written in terms of government, of which king of which tribe was in the ascendency. Yet whereas in the Piscean Age military power more often revolved around a religious figure or evangelistic zeal, during the Arian Age it assuredly and unashamedly did not. That age was more concerned with survival, food production and fecundity, and although religion had its part to play it was to provide a basis of living rather than expansion of influence over neighbours. Military might and expansion took place, of course, but in its own right rather than as a religious takeover or evangelistic crusade.

It is interesting, you note, that the Piscean sign is a feminine sign whilst the Arian sign is a masculine one, and although that roughly categorises and compares religion and warfare in its broadest sense, the religion of the Arian Age was matriarchal and the religions of the Piscean Age were patriarchal!

And now, of course, we are at the dawning of the Age of Aquarius.

The traits of that Age are those of rationalisation, of mental ability, of individualisation, and a degree of perversion. The institutions of State or Church had their place in the previous two great Ages, but have no lasting place in the Age of Aquarius. The individual triumphs, even if it results in a degree of 'shooting oneself in one's own foot'. Small is indeed beautiful for the Age of Aquarius. National and International bodies are secondary. So I wonder what that means for the Church and religion.

Of course time will tell.

15

Natural Cycles

Everything has its time and place and everything is transitory. There are natural cycles to everything from fashion to warfare, politics to national identity, social consideration to garden maintenance to climate change and sea level. Everything changes for Life is change. If it were not so then there would be stagnation or death, but even there the end result is a demonstration of entropy and a dissolving back to constituent parts! Nothing is forever.

That change may only be discernible after a few moments, or it could be hours, days, years, decades, or even centuries, but change there most certainly will be. That is an unchanging fact of life.

Nexialism, even though it may not be an orthodox 'ism', is reputed to be the study of change with regards to society taking into account its politics and religion. Very simply, it postulates that every identifiable and distinct society goes through four stages of development or evolution. It starts with a high degree of energy, expansion and enthusiasm, particularly around individuals – the 'Spring' season, then it evolves into a time of consolidation and steady growth centralising around families or major concerns or business – the 'Summer' season. It then moves into a time of increasing standardisation and lawful pursuit as the legal and traditional minds turn the consolidation into a very stable base – the 'Autumn' season, to eventually fall into a time of rigid adherence and tradition with no room for innovation but falling standards – the 'Winter' season or Fellah time. Such is the way of all empires and civilisations. It is the equivalent of entropy in the physical sciences but seen in social and religious aspects of life. Although there may be attempts to rejuvenate or redirect the society, or sub-groups pair off to start new variations on the theme, the end result is an inevitable decline into exhausted stagnation or death that enables new empires to conquer or assimilate such societies into a grander scheme. Examples of this, although not in chronological order, are Babylon, Egypt, China, Greece, Rome, Maya, Toltec, Aztec, Ceylon and Cambodia, so as the 'Winter' heightened it took a small number of insurgents to bring it down or take it over and the whole process started again.

Each empire had different traits and geographical or sociological prevailing conditions. Each empire had its dominant religion and value system, but in the decline of every empire or society, the integrity that was such a strong aspect of the 'Spring' season gave way to a lowering of standards, hypocrisy, greed and corruption. Seemingly righteous voices might have been motivated by the highest or lowest ideals to stop or pervert the way the society was going, but the outcome was always the same.

I see no difference in the way our own society is going. There have been times of religious revival or national zeal against a common foe that have stemmed the tide again and again. The Renaissance and Reformation revitalised Europe in a profound way. Imperialism and warfare brought in land and wealth that greatly empowered countries and companies and World Wars evoked national identity and pride. Religion was the basis of law and order, civilisation and learning. Evangelism by any means was considered a positive way forward. Indeed the Christian era has stood for far longer than nearly every other society or empire, but I believe its demise is just as sure as all the other lesser ones.

Institutions in the west no longer have the respect of the majority of people. They have become accepted bodies to lay blame or ridicule upon. The traditional expressions of religious persuasion no longer seem to hold the significance that past generations found meaningful, and as a result there are no common standards of decency, integrity and respect that were the cement of society in years gone by. With extended families being very much the rarity, and even the nuclear family breaking down as commitment to a spouse becomes a thing of little worth, then no wonder riots break out, no wonder there is a move for Scotland for the Scots, Britain for the British, Get out of the EU, Deport the immigrants and so on. The soul of the nation is taking a battering and the Church is more often seen as a factor in the decline rather than an answer to it.

It is not that Christianity has had its time – for I believe that Christianity is outside of time, but the Church is no longer a relevant body of expression throughout Europe and North America. It is becoming synonymous with hypocrisy and self-interest, and as I have written of before, I see the death of the Church as being imminent. So more and more people examine their spirituality and see that they are becoming 'spiritual nomads' or religion expressionless Christians – people without a worshipping community to call home.

Such a milieu is a perfect setting for radicalisation from those with the zealous teachings, offering authority and understanding with proven standards to live life by. It only takes a few such voices to convince a larger audience, for that is the nature of the Fellah time. However, after two world wars it is unlikely that a military solution would easily be applied. There is plenty of warfare throughout the world and an escalation of any conflict must remain a possibility, but the United Nations and commercial policies that are in place in the western world produce so many steps to prevent a major conflagration in the west that the likelihood of it happening is slight, despite the many religious prophecies to the contrary and the prophets of doom amongst climatologists and sociologists alike. It is another matter, though, to consider a religious insurgence that makes no claim on the Church's declining influence. Sharia law is but a small step away for some parts of the UK and the New Age philosophy has no central voice or weight anywhere in the land.

I acknowledge that the scenario that I paint is pessimistic and bleak, but I believe it to be a realistic one. What I hope to point out, though, is that radicalisation is not the only way out of a Fellah situation but I need to explore more of Power and in particular the power of the sacred to make my point.

16

Might is Right

What a load of utter rubbish is written about the power of God exercised through religions, and even greater rubbish when it is spoken of as the power of the Sacred! When I hear individuals saying, "God is telling me to do this", or "Jesus is telling me to do that" or "The Lord is telling me to do the other", then I cannot help think that God, Jesus or the Lord are often remarkably lacking in wisdom and uncaring! Yet that is a contradiction in terms, so although I am absolutely sure that God does have a very real power in the world, I am not so sure that it necessarily rests within religious persuasion or prayer as many of the adherents believe. I realise, though, that I need to defend such a statement so let me unpack something of the concept of power to try to get my point across.

Wherever a number of people join forces, for whatever reason, then that group cannot help but have a power in the land. That is true for any group – any group at all. A group may form for any number of reasons, say, the abolition of slavery, or of course to gather together for religious worship. A large number of people in a group demands attention and cannot be ignored, and a religion is essentially just another group of people and so should be considered no differently. However, the power that any group holds does not just depend upon the number of members of the group or how vociferous they are, but the activity that they get up to and the nature of the people themselves as well.

It might be an idea to categorise the types of power by referring to the Kabala symbol. What is revealing is that the categories I use tend to follow the levels of the Kabala from the more basic physical level right through to the spiritual level. It is not in any way imperative that the reader knows anything about the Kabala but it does show how a 'spiritual' body such as the church is more likely to use the tools of the physical and psychological rather than the spiritual in their work in the community.

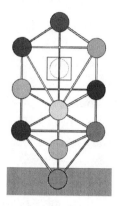

The basic level and the most obvious power is 'Might is right'. But even that comes in different guises. There is a spectrum with one end being the power of the sword or gun whilst, yes, the other end is simply the weight of number of adherents. Somewhere in between is the clamour that they make and, more importantly, the content of that clamour.

Today we have the example of the self-styled Islamic State exhorting the general populace for support. Yes, of course there are many people who see IS as the wonderful liberation from western influence and the return to a true Islamic world order. However, we also see examples in the media of cowed people who are embracing IS, and it is no great leap of intuition to see they have no choice in the matter for they know that to do anything else would be to embrace death.

Stretching back through history we see time after time that control of a nation's religion is a means of controlling the general public of that nation. The Romans had conquered Europe through force of arms and instilled their own brand of religion on the land, and the Druids were executed along with any rallying figure of those times. Which religion was doing God's work in that situation? The expanding Christian religion did the same as IS as it conquered the pagan world in the wake of Pax Romana. Christians used execution against the devil's disciples with the accusation of witchcraft to instil obedience to the church right through to the post-Reformation age. The Crusaders were renowned for their violence and brutality, and even during the great Imperialisation of the world by the European countries and the spread of the Christian message specifically during the Pax Britannica that followed, the gun was considered a civilising tool – and all this done in the name of God! It was an exercise of tremendous power. But to consider it a sacred power is another matter.

And concerning weight of numbers – one training technique in group work is to have all the members of a group 'in the know' yet an individual kept ignorant of the group's intent. The group is to agree with the leader as he or she knocks, say, 11 times on the table and then asks the group how many times was tapped. As the tally goes round the group everyone says 10 times – and provided the member who was ignorant of the intent is towards the end of the tally then he or she usually agrees with the rest of the people. That is the pressure of the peer group, for the individual thinks he or she must be mistaken in order to be in line with the majority decision. And so it is in the case of a large religion. Everyone else cannot possibly be wrong so individuals who otherwise would go in a different religious direction collude with the majority 'vote' for it takes an exceptionally strong person to go against all the neighbours.

17

The Power of Politics

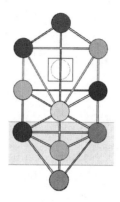

Once again there is a spectrum within political power for the appeal of the politician rests not so much within the published manifesto as to the emotional appeal to the heartstrings of his or her audience. If the politician can hold the moral high ground through earnest or righteous regard then the actual point by point rational argument has little bearing upon the way the vote will go. The shakier the actual ethical point under discussion means the politician needs to exercise a greater degree of projected moral indignation and conviction over the real or imagined injustice of the situation. "God bless you", or "God bless America", tends to be the stock in trade for the North American politician, and the satire against Tony Blair was reflecting a similar trend in the UK when as Prime Minister he was depicted as Saint Tone or an earnest vicar by the TV satirist Harry Enfield.

The political trick is to present the self-interest of the audience in such a way so it doesn't appear to be self-interest at all but in the interest of the general public or majority good. If the politician can divert the audience's scrutiny away from self-regard or the focus of right or wrong into an area of emotional pain or anguish that others may possibly be suffering, and further convince the audience that in fact they will be helping those who suffer by going along with the politician's ideas, then there is no need to think any further.

No doubt goodness has very little to do with the whole thing although the implication is strong that it does.

The Church, or any religion, has a very real advantage therefore when speaking out against a social injustice. It already holds the assumption that it speaks in a prophetic voice that should be obeyed by all. Isn't a churchman or churchwoman supposed to commune with God and so know God's mind on any particular issue? Many a politician would give their right arm for such an advantage from the off. There would be no need to examine any argument or manifesto for, indirectly, God speaks his words of command. Wonderful! Bring on the Food Banks, the NHS and unlimited benefit system, for isn't that helping the poor and needy?

Of course not! But even saying that I acknowledge that I am falling into the same trap of being political, however, I must just say that the NHS was born out of an altruistic vision but today it is almost universally admitted that it has now become an ogre that is out of control. No longer are benefits considered a benefit but a right, and the NHS financial pot is empty or in the red. No matter what your political persuasion or your faith or your moral regard, if there is no more money in the pot then it cannot be given to anyone, let alone the poor and needy. Yes, of course there are people who need the community's compassion and help with disability allowance and professional care, but to my mind the Church of England's bandwagon report of "Who is my neighbour?" parodies the parable of the Good Samaritan. The Samaritan helped the victim who had fallen amongst thieves, he also promised the innkeeper to reimburse any expense that would still be needed to help the victim to full recovery, but he didn't offer the victim a blank cheque for the rest of his life. As the founder of the 'Big Issue' put it, a 'hand up' is needed rather than a 'handout'. Social care and the defence of the realm is never a simplistic endeavour as the church report suggests.

Religion most certainly has a prophetic ministry to the people and it is the conscience to the nations. People such as Elijah and Isaiah were seemingly heavily caught up in politics, but if the social crusade is the be all and end all of religious ministry and the overwhelming motivation of the leaders of a religion then that is a view I find abhorrent in the extreme. No, obviously not the option or action of helping the poor and needy but the usurping of authority and an abuse of positional power that a dog collar or special clothing sometimes brings. When I read in the national press that the Church of England was preparing a guide on what the church members should consider before voting in a General Election then it seemed to me that the Church was taking an extremely large step far too far. When the Archbishop of Canterbury apologises to the German people for the bombing of Dresden without any remit from the British people to do so then that only makes me boil in indignation. Who is this unelected person who speaks on my behalf? Perhaps the Church should stop playing politics and start praying in earnest, for although once again we see the exercise of considerable power it cannot be considered the power of the sacred nor is it generally clear what the right or wrong of a given situation is. Hence the need for debate rather than diktat.

18

Psychological Shenanigans

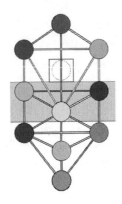

No doubt I am missing many other ways of regarding power than what I am describing here, however, at this level of regard I can see two distinct types of power exercised by individuals and groups alike that are irrevocably linked, that of emotional need and of rational identification.

It is a small step from the emotional game-playing in politics, often pandering to a synthetic need of an audience that fits the desired outcome of the politician (usually the politician's desire to stay in power!), to the fulfilling of an actual emotional need that is recognised as such by the recipient. Gratitude to the supplier is one obvious response, but so also is the need to respond in some way.

This is different to the previous political machination, for in that case the politician was very much in control, getting you the voter to vote his way or add your name to his or her cause. It might appear as if I am splitting hairs but whereas the politician makes use of you in some way the exercise of psychological power is more at your choice or disposal. At the psychological level it is recognising that the need is real and actual and belongs to you. Up to that point the need might not have been realised, or if it was known it might have been denied, but once the need has been accepted then something further is required – means of supplying that need, of assuaging its clamour or demand. Avoidance is no longer an option.

The need can be varied and found in a social cause; a needful relationship; or a revelation of spiritual life. It doesn't need to be of any special kind to be psychological in nature. It is the person's acceptance of that need that defines its place and how the need is supplied that shows the power exercised as being sacred or otherwise.

Loneliness is a curse of western society. As the populace has become more mobile and moved in the seeking of employment, then families and communities have broken up. As traditional ties have declined in strength and meaning then traditional wisdom and means of help has also ebbed away. Single parent families are more often the norm and lonely pensioners now a way of life. The sense of belonging and having roots has been lost. Individuals have been thrust onto their own resources, more often failing in the attempt. So when a group opens their doors to the unloved or lonely, then there is a very strong attraction for the lonely to join.

When a church does the same thing then I begin to question the motivation and integrity of the church elders, although it is an acceptable entre into the worshipping community.

Some churches are no more than a club for a particular class or type of person. If your face fits then you are welcome to join, but if your manner, dress, colour or financial status is so obviously different to the rest of the congregation, then the discomfort will be forever present and become an obstacle to full membership. Groups within the group may be formal such as Young Wives, Youth Club, Choir and PCC but the cliques and sub-groups will abound whenever disparity is around. Are you 'in' with the 'in crowd'?

I cannot help wonder at times what the motivation of the evangelist may be or of the integrity of the style of evangelism taken. Of course an evangelist may be inspired by God to preach to the people. That is an accepted and very necessary ministry of the Church, but if the evangelist is playing the numbers game and includes a financial collection to carry out the work of God, then a certain degree of cynicism enters the equation and I challenge the motivation of that preacher. If the evangelist promotes the need for repentance and yet the listener had no conscious need to repent, then what is this thing called guilt that is pounced upon and the solution produced like a conjurer pulling a rabbit out of a hat. I doubt the validity of that kind of conversion. If the context of the preaching played heavily on the evoking of an emotional response then I challenge the integrity of the 'performers' or supporters. As I understand it, the listener must be free to choose to respond or not rather than dance as a puppet to the preachers' tune. What lasting good is the response if it is mindless or just reactive in nature. A true conversion is a conscious decision as a consequence to a recognised need to repent and change one's lifestyle.

There are other psychological factors that bear upon the need to belong. To be a big fish in a small pond gives a sense of worth that may not be possible within the greater community or neighbourhood. To have that recognised by the group by wearing a kind of uniform called vestments, or holding a symbol of office such as a church warden's staff or a dog collar fulfils the psychological need to 'be a somebody'. To cloak the proceedings in ritual gives a sense of the dramatic and invocation of the mysterious. These are serious tools in the art of worship and although some people have turned their collective backs on ritual, such as the Quakers, others such as the Orthodox Churches and Roman Catholicism have taken it to the extreme. Even silence can be a binding force, whilst the very name of Communion describes the situation or desired outcome.

To belong to a tribe means embracing the tribal religion. To belong to a church is accepting a constitution of faith – or at least paying lip service to it. But beneath the surface psychological ins and outs there is hoped to be an underlying commitment to God – of whatever religion is being followed. This is the point when the psychological power begins to give ground to the sacred and spiritual – at last!

19

Inspirational Power

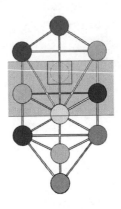

What is often forgotten in today's more secular society is the awesome influence of religion at the very heart of a nation. The soul of the UK nation is being eroded by pornography, licence, violence, and selfish greed and the residue of depression or social ills is apparent on every newscast. The Church has not been slow to point the finger of blame at government ministerial level for surely one of its roles is to be the conscience of the Nation. However, what is seldom grasped is that the Church also has a responsibility to stop the rot from taking place. What is not realised is that religion has so often been the catalyst, patron, and inspiration behind the treasures of art and poetry throughout the world that lifts the spirit and evokes deep archetypal responses when read, heard or viewed.

Our legal system, creaking and open to abuse, grew out of religious law. Our monarchy, so often shrouded in paternalistic mystery or celebrity status, has been intertwined with religion from its earliest days. And Remembrance Day services resonate with a nation's need to salute heroism, patriotism, and the ultimate sacrifice by thousands in the past.

Of course art does not have to be dependent upon religion, but so often in the past it has only been the church or the religion of the day that could afford to commission a work of art. The Renaissance was a time of secularising art and knowledge, of rediscovering the creative nature of mankind outside of religion and understanding the world with mankind rather than God at its centre, but such a period has tended to be the exception rather than the rule.

Music stirs the soul whether it is a religious work or not. But when the motivation of the composer is to convey something of such deep meaningful appreciation of life then no matter what the stated belief system of the composer is or that of the listener in turn, there is usually a response that defies words and somehow resonates with the higher functions of the mind, inspiring the listener to respect, awe or even spiritual experience. The fact that it is usually of a religious or spiritual nature in the first place means that the response is usually in accord with the intention of the composer, resonating with similar feelings held by the composer that the composer has endeavoured to convey.

Neither is it a transitory response. The same music will evoke similar feelings again and again, each time it is played or heard. Tears may flow or the heart beat faster and thought put on hold in anticipation of the expected inner stirrings, and experience is personal and not easily put aside. People can be struck dumb and have no words to express beauty when it is presented in visual form. Others may speak at length in an erudite fashion, but the experience is still a thing that is essentially private and cumulative.

Poetry is able to reach beyond the words that are actually used to touch upon the mysteries of the soul that could not normally be spoken about, and as there are demons as well as angels within the subconscious, figuratively speaking, then the listener may just as likely be disturbed as uplifted. Nature has a power to inspire or to frighten, and not just by a display of abnormal weather or natural catastrophe. The beautiful sunrise or sunset, the double rainbow or cosmic comet shower display, the scent and sight of a rose in bloom, all have a power to uplift a flagging spirit and all without a religion in sight. This is a kind of 'power of the sacred' or at least a power of the subtle that invariably is claimed by a religion of one kind or another but it can just as easily stand outside of any religious setting. It is an evocation beyond the conscious choice of religious constitution or creed and can be utilised by the religious or non-religious alike, or by any religious person claiming their deity as Creator.

20

Symbols

It is said "a picture is worth a thousand words". Indeed, at any one time there is more information being gathered by a person through the eyes than by any of the other senses. Of course we ignore those other senses at our peril, but putting all the data together from ears, skin, tongue and nose, it still does not even begin to approach the volume of data being received from our eyes. Humankind is essentially a visually communicating animal, and the relative sizes of the processing equipment in our brains reflect the significance of images over sounds and feelings.

A picture in itself is nothing more than a collection of lines and colours upon a surface or medium that depicts an experience in life. It can be a real life picture or an abstract one. It can be a photograph or a drawing incorporating 'poetic license' to convey extra meaning. However, it is at that point the picture begins to become a symbol, as well as a replicating photograph, for a symbol is a picture of some kind or other with extra layers of meaning.

It is the extra 'something' that evokes feelings or memory instinctively over and above the obvious visual imagery. For example, a picture of a naked woman may remain just an 'aide memoir' of a particular woman and situation or it may become a means of evoking desire, lust or love. Indeed without such an evocation of a scantily clad woman most advertisements would lack any power of enticement to buy! However, it is not just desire that could be evoked. Anger or feelings of degradation are just as likely to be experienced by some people. It may also be the case on occasions that all 'lower' emotions are transcended by the sight of great beauty which take the receptor to a height of awareness that can only be talked of in religious terms. That is the power of symbols appreciated over and above the actual image perceived.

Jung suggested that in the subconscious, surface symbols, those nearest the conscious awareness, relate to the personal experiences of that individual. They hold meaning just for that individual. The symbols come into being there because of the more unusual, traumatic or repeated experiences that the individual undergoes, and form in the subconscious without plan or will or intent. They arise through life's experiences and cannot be exorcised by force or strength of will – they just are.

Jung goes on to say that at the deepest level of the inner mind are the archetypes. These are the building blocks of consciousness that are common to all human kind. They are there because the person is a human being and alive! The archetypes are the universal mental counterpart to the universal descriptive parts of the physical body, and cannot be thought of as *not* being there as we cannot think of a person without a head, liver or lungs. They are not put into the mind after birth, like the individual symbols, but are there in the womb, in the genes, in the spirit.

The most important part to remember about archetypes is that they are not quiet, having no part to play in the person's life. They are working all the time and they do not have to be taught to the individual. They just are, in exactly the same way as the brain works, the lungs work or the eyes work. A person does not have to be taught how to breathe or to see – they just get on with breathing or seeing, so the universal symbols are there and work automatically all the time, for good or ill.

In between the two extremes are the depths of subconscious that relate to the ethnic psyche. It is at the ethnic level that the archetypes can begin to be appreciated, or their power felt, for at the deepest level of mind the actual description or concept of that archetype slips away between the fingers of understanding to a deeper level yet. You can never actually get hold of an archetype in itself, but need a vehicle to hold it and express it, giving it form and conceptual placement.

For example, the archetype of 'The Hero' is undoubtedly a universal concept translated into many, many stories and sagas throughout the world. The concept can easily be understood – but in its respective settings. So you have the Samurai warrior of the Far East; the Viking Hero earning his place in the halls of Valhalla; William Tell of Central Europe and Arthur or Robin Hood in these lands. However, to try to describe the quality and concept of the 'Hero' without the setting and subtlety of under-standing of place and time dooms the description to failure. The setting is absolutely necessary. The setting is the ethnic placing, and consists of ethnic symbols or psyche, and just like the universal or archetypal symbols, these are not learnt but have their part within the inner person through the group experiences or group mind, and are born to that person by virtue of that person's genetic history.

Two rather unusual consequences or corollaries are that, as the ethnic symbols grow over the years due to the collective experiences of the tribe or area, then the symbols always tend to be out of date or behind the times, being depicted as historical figures, old-fashioned buildings or fairy stories and folk tales. The issues they relate to may be completely up to date, but the imagery used is from the past. It is only the individual symbols that may be contemporary. It is as if the current individual symbols, en masse, become the next generation's ethnic symbols, gradually sinking into the inner sphere as time passes, becoming more clan than individual, then more ethnic than clan, and so on. Perhaps that is the way the mental building blocks evolve, just as the physical body has its mechanisms in place in order to adapt, change or evolve over the years.

The further unusual consequence is that an individual of any ethnic group may have religious symbols within their psyche that they may consciously never subscribe to – or even vehemently object to. Remember the religious belief system belongs to the conscious mind, but symbols belong to the subconscious. It is the group mind and experience that has given rise to the group or ethnic symbol, for it was the group consensus of belief and expectation that gave rise to experience in the past. Thus it is beyond an individual's strength or ability ever to exorcise an ethnic symbol just because they do not believe in it. The belief systems do not control the subconscious.

Ethnicity is therefore a very important part of the power of the sacred, for the intensity of response that the symbols evoke will be greater the closer they are to the person's own ethnicity.

21

Psychic Sensitivity and Influence

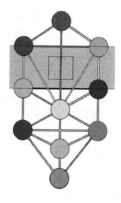

In Genesis Chapter 1, verse 31, we read that in God's eyes his creation was "good". That is one understatement of understatements, for our minds cannot really begin to appreciate the harmony and immensity of the whole of creation even when taking into account the very blinkered sight of things that we do. Even though our study and research in the macrocosm of our physical, sociological and psychological environment keeps pace with a similar earnest and accelerating voyage of discovery of our microcosmic environment, the view remains so narrow. The interaction and interplay between these two great realms are only just beginning to be appreciated, but as the rapidly special-ising fields of study often fail in their desire not to lose track of each other's advances this interaction is more likely being guessed than understood.

Take, for example, the physical world with its cacophony of sound and signals bombarding the senses of man. Have you ever tried to listen and be aware of every sound coming to your ears? The noise of the traffic outside, the refrigerator working, birds singing, someone talking, the radio playing etc. All these noises come to a person's ears yet the brain chooses to listen or focus upon only one or two of those signals. All the rest become shunted away as background noise. Perhaps the person is even totally unaware of any noise due to the familiarity of the signal input. Also, notice, the most random signal conveys the most information or is of relative importance to its surroundings. For example, the slight new rattle heard in the car draws instant attention, yet after a while it becomes lost in the general noise associated with normal running. A flashing light in the midst of darkness is instantly noticed, yet a flashing light amidst many others is just one of a crowd and not worthy of comment.

So thinking of all the masses of signal input just associated with sound, the brain chooses to be aware of only one or two signals, usually the loudest or most unusual, but it hears the lot. Yet these unnoticed or subliminal sounds may have an effect without conscious awareness of the person involved. Such sounds may be the hypnotic timekeeping of a metronome, the ticking of a clock, or the bass drum rhythm of a band, orchestra or pop group. Tell the person that they were tapping their foot or even breathing in time with the beat and they will not believe you. Draw their attention to it as they continue and they will be mildly astonished or annoyed.

Nor must we limit sound impinging upon the ears of that person as the only way the person can appreciate that stimulus, for the whole person is in one aspect a sense organ. It is just that some parts of the body react more strongly to particular stimuli than other parts. So, for example, the larger surface area of the body, the chest and abdomen rather than the ears, more often feels the lowest frequencies of sound that people 'hear'.

Sound, of course, is only a minute portion of all the signals impinging upon the person. Even more bewildering, and possibly frightening, is the range and effect of the electromagnetic spectrum. Not only is the hypnotic and subliminal effects observed in the range of frequencies we term light but each individual appreciates these particular frequencies differently. Just as each person has his or her own individual response pattern to sound stimuli, i.e., we cannot all hear the lowest or highest frequencies and we even experience middle frequencies with differing strengths, so we each experience light in our own way.

Display a white light spectrum and ask individuals to mark particular colours, the strongest or brightest colour and the limits of the spectrum seen. The results may show that sometimes a band of colour is marked which in reality belongs more to the infrared or ultra violet frequencies, and so is invisible to the majority of people. I am sure this is the likely reason why some people can "see" the Life Field or aura (the detectable and measurable electromagnetic field around living bodies) while the majority of people cannot see anything beyond the skin. The 'psychic' sight in this case becomes just an abnormal extension of normal vision and can surely be no more thought of as being a gift of the devil as can colour blindness be considered a curse of the same.

When one begins to consider the tremendous range of signals impinging, then it is little wonder that individuals experience and appreciate creation in their individualistic way. The vast majority may experience and interpret signals similarly, perhaps in nearly identical ways, but there are inevitably a few who are aware of signals that the majority are unaware of. The more radical the difference of experience it is the less likely it is to occur, and thus the more individual in awareness and interpretation it becomes. Such an awareness is the realm of the psychic. So like any other talent psychic gifts are more pronounced in some people than in others yet found in most people, and they may be as varied in manifestation as are people's abilities to comprehend, adore, produce, or shun music in its widest sense.

We are truly now entering the realms of the power of the sacred, for awareness of the subtle and influence within the same is the nuts and bolts of any religion.

22

The Setting

Although the most usual way of describing the countryside is in terms of topography, geology, fauna and flora, the whole world can be described in energetic terms as well, something that is only now being considered again in this society. It is possible to describe how the life-fields around every living thing interact with each other and with the land upon which they dwell. If you could actually see, clairvoyantly, the energy flow as a living movement it would be similar to the flow of early morning fog or mist as it flows down valleys and dissipates in the sunshine but also vibrant and full of colour. Then you would appreciate the world in a most wondrous fashion. New features would appear of soaring columns, up-welling flows or moving slopes of energy; new colours and intensities that defeat description; and you would also see repeated patterns of that energy flow, again and again. Whilst some of these patterns would seem to follow no physical counterpart, others surround manmade features.

Everything interacts with everything else, but some things are more positive in their effects, building up a stronger picture and supporting each feature of the general scene, while others are much less helpful or constructive. Natural flows of water or rock outcrops tend to dominate the energy picture, pushing or pulling the energy flow one way or another. This energy flow may seem to stream out of the ground due to a particular mineral wealth in that area, be caught in an energy vortex that is sucked into a stream or river, or simply dissipate like a morning mist as it hovers over a sea of sand or water. Trees may stream forth energy 'particles' like sparkling, darting fire-flies. Forests may flood the land. Lines of energy usually criss-cross an area. It is never a static place, for energy flows from a higher potential to a lower one; different energies from different energy sources having different effects upon each other, the land and on Life. It is an exciting place to be, caught up in the warp and weft of Life.

Humankind may think it necessary to build a road that crosses the land, and this will affect the energy picture. What it is constructed of, as well as its dimensions and gradient, all have their part to play. It may seem obvious but the wider the road the greater the impact it will have on the energy environment. The more a contour is followed the less the impact will be. The straighter the line, the more it pulls energy along in its direction. A tunnel or cutting may have disastrous consequences. Hedges and field boundaries may be full of Life, bringing a summation or culmination of tiny individual effects to the general whole, usually of a positive influence. Railway tracks and electricity lines crossing the land cut the energy fields in majestic style, but usually with a negative influence.

And threading their way through all of this are lines of energy that follow no manmade structure. Some of these are perfectly straight, while others meander in sinuous style. The result just of these is a network of lines that radiate and carry energy from one place to another – a system that has a direct effect upon the health and occupation of all creatures of the land – seen and unseen. An effect that is usually one of ensuring good health as the Life giving energy is spread upon the countryside.

The straight lines are called ley lines or geopathic stress lines. These can be both natural and manmade, however, at the moment let me liken them to the energy meridians of the human body. They are the meridians of the Earth Body or Gaia. If you could use your clairvoyant sight you would notice that where an obstacle lies upon the ley the energy is correspondingly changed. Sometimes the effect is to strengthen the line, sometimes a new line is produced; sometimes ripples of energy radiate out from the obstacle; sometimes the energy is pulled into new shapes or even changes its colour or frequency! Obviously one would need to understand the nature of the obstacle and the corresponding effect if one was to be able to manipulate the energy to some particular end. Generally it seems that buildings seem to disrupt the flow or use the energy, depending upon whether the builders knew what they were doing. Trees mainly radiate the energy, whilst standing stones either focus the energy line or radiate it out in a similar way as does a tree.

You would also notice that often where natural lines cross that point has been marked in some way. A standing stone may well have two, three or even more lines intersecting at that point. In the past someone decided to delineate that point. He or she must have been aware of the concentration of energy and found it helpful if that spot was acknowledged, guarded, enhanced or whatever. Remember the energy is real, as will be the effect and not every effect is guaranteed to work as desired. There will be many side effects that suddenly appear for no apparent reason that you know of.

Remember also that the manmade ley line system of today's Europe, with its corresponding circles of stones and avenues, was constructed at a time when Life was much more a matter of survival than it is today. Yet an awful amount of time and physical energy went into the construction of a 'national grid' of their times, so it is imperative to understand why. It is not that energy was being drawn around the land just for the sake of manipulation, but to produce a healthy flow of life giving energy to encourage fecundity, variety and a balance in the ecology to an area of land that would otherwise be struggling. That was a way of staving off hardship! Just as in a desert environment, despite the initial tremendous investment, it is a lifesaving project to bring water to the land through canals and sluices. So a land that is needful of healthy plants and animals can be given a similar boost of fecundity through the ley system, despite the capital layout of the day.

The religion of the day in those times long past, meant a far closer identification with Nature, in all its phases, dangers and harvest delights. The priesthood of that religion had to be able to produce the 'goods', especially if the people depended upon them for their continuing life and community. The religion, the community and the way of life would not survive unless the religion worked. The religion and the science of the day were really one and the same thing.

As I said before, ethnicity is a very important part of the power of the sacred for the intensity of response that the symbols evoke will be greater the closer they are to the person's own ethnicity. So the setting, with its construction, buildings, atmosphere, and overall ambience will be a major factor in the psychic sensitivity and influence in that place. The closer the setting is to the individual's ethnic roots, the greater the evocation or response called forth. Here the power of the sacred interacts with the religious settings of both past ages and present expression. The religion must work for there to be adherents. A religion is not just a political movement with a bit of theatre thrown in for good measure, giving opportunity to dress up and pontificate. It is not just a moral code for a society to live by. A religion must have a power to change lives for the good and to influence the unseen powers and subtle energies that it purports to understand. It must be an authority on things spiritual. To do anything else is to live a lie, even if most of its adherents do not understand the core principles of its workings, of prayer, grace, blessings and curses. Somewhere beneath all the ritual, theatre and hype it must deliver the goods – or be exposed as a sham and die.

23

The level of the Unseen – Invisible and Sacred

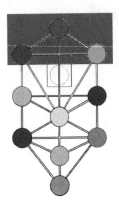

The Christian Nicene Creed of Belief states "...I believe in the visible and the invisible...", and inevitably the difficulty begins in defining what is meant by "invisible". Already in one sense I have written about invisible forces for, strictly speaking, sound is a material wave (the "sound" bouncing from molecule to molecule), but nuclear, gravity and electromagnetic forces belong to the non-material world and are quite invisible. They are non-material qualities although they have considerable effect upon the material world. For that reason they are generally considered part of the "physical" world and could be classified under "visible" for the purpose of stating belief. The invisible refers to the realms of the spirit and subtle forces, the non-material world and its inhabitants as described in the Bible and believed and experienced by countless numbers of religious and non-religious alike.

The Greek word 'psyche' has an ambiguity in translation that causes the terms 'soul' and 'spirit' to render an inconsistency in the biblical use of the word. Similarly the Hebrew word 'ruach' is variously translated 'spirit', 'wind' or 'breath', so for example in Ezekiel: 37v9 and 37v14 all three translations are required. Again in John: 3v6 the corresponding Greek word 'pneuma' is used with a deliberate play on words which can only be kept in an English translation by a marginal note to say that the word for 'wind' is the same as that translated 'spirit'. Above all, the term spirit is applied to the bodiless Holy Spirit of God, e.g., John: 3v6 "That which is born of the spirit is spirit", and again John: 4v24 "God is spirit...". This is the unseen or invisible spoken of in the Creed.

Similarly the Bible refers to beings that are spirit just as the realms in which they live are spirit. Job: 1. 6; 2. 1; 38. 7 refers to them as 'sons of God', while Matthew: 22. 30 calls them 'angels'. This latter word actually describes one of their duties, for both the Hebrew and Greek words mean messengers. Hebrews: 1. 14 "what are they all (angels) but ministrant spirits sent out to serve for the sake of those who are to inherit salvation". Unfortunately in the Bible there is equal reference not only to angels and messengers sent from God, but also to evil spirits or demons and devils and our need to stand and fight against them, e.g., Ephesians: 6. 12; Mark: 9. 17ff.

Theologians might speak of Communion with God or being At One with God or God within or the Holy Spirit within. Psychologists might talk of Angels and Demons within and Exorcists talk of Angels and Demons without. Occultists also refer to spirit beings, although not with the same clear distinctions between their good or evil intentions as found in the scriptures. Such names as Spirit Guides, Divas, Elves, Fairies, Undines etc., describe their appearance and functions, and when we assume that there is interaction between the visible and invisible or spiritual realms and the participants knowingly encourage this by various means, then there may be reason to be cautious of psychic sensitivity and talents.

In this case, if I may be permitted to use what is for some people a rather picturesque style of language, such gifts may indeed be not so much Devil given but Devil inspired and enhanced. Even more fearful is the situation when evidence suggests manipulation is taking place directed from either the visible or invisible realms on a subliminal or subconscious level, to the detriment of all concerned.

However, as we hear this argument repeated time and again in Church type circles for reasons to avoid psychic sensitivity, this logically allows the more attractive situation also to exist, i.e., that such gifts may be good or God inspired and enhanced, and help is taking place from either realm or both realms, consciously or subconsciously, to the *good* of all concerned. If we accept one to be the case we must logically allow the other in our belief system.

This interaction and influence, consciously or unconsciously, is nothing other than the power of the sacred pure and simple for it takes place at the spiritual or unseen invisible level of being, either within the person's psyche or subconscious or outside of it from separate discarnate beings. Take your choice!

24

Is the power of the Sacred transferrable as a Spiritual Gift?

A gift, by definition, is something given by one person to another. It is not something earned or worked for as a reward, it is something freely given that can be used, misused, not used or abused by the person receiving the gift. If conditions were laid upon the receiver by the donor then it would be in the form of a grant and not a gift. If the receiver abuses or misuses the gift then the relationship between the two can be strained to breaking point, but a gift once given is not something that can be taken back.

In the same way a spiritual gift is not earned and can be used, not used, misused or abused. If it is used wisely and in keeping with the ethics of the religion then the relationship grows between the receiver and the donor. If the gift is misused or not used or abused then the relationship will suffer – and in this case we are talking about spirituality.

St Paul, in his first letter to Corinthians in chapter 12 writes about the gifts of the Spirit, giving a list of some of those gifts, and in his letter to Galatians chapter 5 he writes about the fruit of the Spirit and similarly gives a list of some of the types of fruit of the Spirit. So it is seen that although a gift may be given, how it is used will determine whether the fruit will grow and mature – that is spirituality.

A spiritual being, therefore, constitutes a non-physical living entity or a citizen of the unseen realms. Added to this there is normally an understanding of intrinsic goodness or holiness associated with such a being, but obviously that is not always and necessarily the case. Neither is there an automatic conferring of wisdom upon a discarnate spirit.

A spiritual force would constitute a non-physical influence upon the physical or mental areas of life that is directed in some way by another being, and not necessarily by a spiritual being. Such force has traditionally been thought of as prayer, healing, blessing, cursing or ill wishing, magic or the like, and the ability to manipulate a spiritual force, either consciously or unconsciously, would therefore be inextricably linked in some way to spirituality or spiritual maturity, by its application, intensity, wholesomeness, goodness (or otherwise) and outcome. This cannot be understated.

Although every religion would like to claim the monopoly of such manipulation and power of the sacred, it is also just as obvious that such things are not the prerogative of any single religion, ethic or philosophy, but common to all to some degree or other, for these are the arrows and balm of the spirit realms rather than just wishful states of mind induced by the hearing of certain words of comfort or anger. Blessings and curses have a spiritual reality in that they have a power to affect the visible and invisible realms. As I have said before they are the nuts and bolts of all religions.

To help keep the distinction between the spiritual and psychic or mental realms and the abilities associated with either, I like to use the word 'talent' to describe the natural ability that a person may be born with that can be developed or otherwise as the person sees fit – that is rather than the word 'gift'. I know they are usually considered to be synonymous but to my way of thinking a gift is something spiritual and given and so later conferred upon a person rather than that person being born with it. I acknowledge that talents themselves are God given but I like to see that as only in the sense that everything about that person's DNA is also God given, and although both talents and gifts are things that are given that can be used, misused or abused, gifts can be given to people at any time of life to be used straightaway without preamble or hours spent in development – unlike a talent.

You may think I am splitting hairs or wasting time in word play but it does alter the way a person may be perceived as they exercise their gift or talent and how it affects their spirituality.

Inspiration

Take for example the gift of Inspiration. This is different from the power of inspiration that I have already written about. In that case it was a general response to art, music, heroism and 'star presence' that could inspire people to view the world around them in a higher or altruistic light, to make an effort to emulate or make a difference to society to the good of all. It was a response to an unspecified call.

The gift of Inspiration, however, is an ability to change specific individuals by a personal or direct approach. It doesn't have to be by appeal, preaching or dialogue, although this is so often the route, but could be by prayer, blessing, cursing or subtle and possibly insidious influence from a distance. Even without saying a word a charismatic leader can enter a room and by their very presence dominate the thinking taking place there – for good or ill. The leader may be using a natural talent that has taken years to develop, being en rapport with associates, but the associates are given the gift of being uplifted or inspired to greater things in that moment of time.

The 'ministering spirits' as written about in the New Testament "Letter to Hebrews", chapter 1, undoubtedly makes use of inspiration to assist in the serving of God. I am sure that for the most part this is received unknowingly but it does not rule out the occasional times when the recipient is in full awareness of the 'otherness' of the source of ideas. However, so many people who are in need of psychiatric care can also hear voices! In the latter instance I am sure that such voices are generally from the angels and demons within the person's own subconscious rather than from an external source, but am I equally sure that that is not so in every case. My time as an exorcist showed that people who were disruptive and subsequently exorcised would invariably calm down and behave in a more normal rational way.

Glossolalia, often understood among Protestant Christians as speaking in tongues, is the fluid vocalising of speech-like syllables that lack any readily comprehended meaning, in some cases as part of regular religious practice. It may sound like a real language – it might even be a real language of men or angels – but it is not understood as such by the person praying. It is explained as the person letting go of their rational mind and voice and letting the Holy Spirit speak through them. It is sometimes accompanied by the gift of Interpretation of Tongues, where a second person takes up the thread of prayer and gives a subsequent prayerful interpretation, but both gifts are most certainly gifts of Inspiration as given by the Spirit of God – the power of the sacred.

Spiritualists and New Agers are conversant with the gift of Inspiration as explained by 'channelling'. In this case a person is able to go into a trance state and let a discarnate being speak to others by using the vocal chords of the person under trance. As such it lies somewhere between Glossolalia and Possession for the person under trance willingly submits to the 'overshadowing' and could, in most instances, stop the process by deliberate will. Hopefully there is no lasting influence for good or ill, leaving the person to continue with their own walk through life making their own decisions and mistakes rather than carrying out other people's machinations.

Gifts of healing

The gifts of healing are not confined to the medical profession, to alternative therapies or prayer intercession. The gifts of healing are best described as when a needful person receives the 'laying on of hands', 'chrism oil' or similar symbols of given help either in prayer or therapeutic session and without the intervention of chemical or physical influence and where the recipient improves in their well-being or health. There is much spoken of to explain the process but most of it sounds like mumbo-jumbo of the first order. Energies, Angels, higher orders, resonance, other dimensions, Guides, Avatars, giving the Light, Balancing, soul realignment, and so on and so on are all used in a mix or combination to cover pet theories or fashionable ideas. However it might be explained the observation is that certain people are able to help needful people by touch and willpower in a giving, channelling or prayer attitude. It is an exercise of power that is only explained when the subtle and unseen, the spiritual, is invoked in some way or other.

Knowledge and Wisdom

Gifts that defy explanation using conventional understanding are the gifts of knowledge and the gifts of wisdom. They are not synonymous.

The gift of knowledge is just that – being able to draw knowledge of a fact out of thin air, so to speak. It has been taught as an esoteric talent to extend the natural ability to memorize a vast amount of facts and figures and let unconscious scanning or the slumbering subconscious draw the relevant facts out of memory upon demand. I am sure that is one explanation and ability but it is not the gift of knowledge as I understand it. The gift is when a person, without prior feeding of facts, can 'know' about a situation or fact and pronounce upon it with authority. The person 'knows' it is true. Whether the person is receiving the knowledge by inspiration from another being or finding out directly is a moot point, but somewhere between the concepts of talent and gift a technique can be used to direct the person in visualisation to find out the facts of a situation by visiting a 'virtual' library or 'the Akashic Records' within their own subconscious.

Similarly the gift of wisdom is 'knowing' how best to act in any particular situation. Whether the facts of a situation are explored or sought after is not necessary in order to come to a decision as to how to act. It is not an extension of earthly wisdom for earthly wisdom is an accumulation of experience of life's rich pattern. The best way forwards, coming from exercising the gift of wisdom, may be without understanding motivation and consequence. It is an answer given in the moment – such is the nature of a gift.

Prayer

I include the gift of prayer in this essay for not everyone is seemingly able to pray deeply. We are taught that God hears our prayers whoever is praying, but some people undoubtedly have a ministry of prayer whilst others feel they are 'praying' to a brick wall. Those who have the gift feel compelled to pray. They do not even need to communicate in words or lengthy phrases but in the communion with the Spirit there is an understanding of committing to God, even in silence, the situation which needs to be prayed about. It is a joining of the person's spirit with the Spirit of God. It is possibly just a groaning with concerns too deep for words (Romans 8.26) *We do not know what we ought to pray for, but the Spirit himself intercedes for us through wordless groans.*

Apostolic succession!

A spiritual gift does not have to be given by God!

The Old Testament prophet who has more recorded stories of psychic or supernatural nature accredited to him than any other person is Elisha. He displays abilities such as predicting the future with complete accuracy (e.g. 2 Kings: 7. 18, 19, 200), which was a requirement that *had* to be fulfilled in order to be recognised as being a prophet of the Lord (Deuteronomy: 18.22). He knew what was happening at a distance by perhaps clairvoyance or clairaudience (2 Kings: 8. 12) or even by astral travelling (2 Kings: 5. 26). He performed miracles (e.g., 2 Kings: 4. 1; 7. 41, 42, 44; 6. 6, 7); healings (2 Kings: 4. 31, 37; 5. 14); curses (2 Kings: 4. 27; 6. 18). What is rather surprising is that although he most certainly saw spiritual beings he was also able to pass this gift on to his servant (2 Kings: 6. 17).

The ability to sense water and other buried or hidden materials is very common. It is estimated that nearly one third of all people can do this (dowsing) but few seldom do. But a strange way of facilitating this ability in others is for an experienced dowser to lay a hand upon a non-dowser as they try to dowse and somehow this quickens the ability in the other person. Once the non-dowser finds they can in fact dowse then the ability stays with that person even when the experienced dowser removes their hand. Not every experienced dowser can do this but for those who can it is a form of commissioning or laying on of hands that passes on that gift or talent afresh.

Taking things that little bit further, it is a small jump to see how this passing on of gifts can be ritualised in various rites of initiation or ordination such as the laying on of hands in the Church of England rite of Confirmation or the initiation rite of Healing in Reiki, and within the Christian church theorised as the apostolic succession or passing on of 'spiritual gifts' that are part and parcel of leadership of the church. One wonders, however, if the potential giver of the gift actually has the ability to pass it on in the first place and if so with what gift or gifts they believe they are commissioning the church member! It may look like an automatic or mechanical act within the rite like 'turning on a tap of grace' or a bit of theatre but the spiritual reality of it all may be somewhat debateable. Just because the outward acts and prayerful words are sincerely spoken or enacted doesn't necessarily make the inward and hidden power a reality.

Whatever the gift

Whatever the gift or talent, such sensitivity or working of the talent is the basis of *all* sacred experience, no matter what religion it refers to. It should also be the basis of all spiritual experience, but sometimes that experience is clouded by religious expectation (see next essay) but the whole range of psychic and spiritual phenomena are the nuts and bolts of all religions, otherwise the teachings of prayer and spiritual gifts, spirituality and life after death are nothing more than empty words, a sham or hoax to convince the gullible of other worldly status and happenings and a means of maintaining a less than worthy power base in the community. Surely that is absolutely unthinkable, even if the perpetrators are taken in by their own hype and propaganda!

25

How does it Work?

Because of what has already been said in the essay 'Psychic Sensitivity and Influence', first it might be best to ponder as to whether an experience can more easily be ascribed to the psychic (mental) or to the spiritual, or whether the experience comes from within the person him or herself or from the spiritual realms. The complexity of the situation is perhaps best described by the use of one or two examples.

One such is the ministry of preaching which is often described as a gift from God or as a natural talent. One would find it very difficult to say exactly how such a ministry is exercised and to say where the natural ability of the speaker is overshadowed by the inspiration of the Holy Spirit. Paul writes that the gift of preaching is given as a gift of the Holy Spirit to the Church. It is something above or beyond man's natural talents to instruct and edify the same. Not everyone is a preacher and we can see that Paul is quite correct in that not every naturally good speaker is necessarily a good preacher. That does not mean preachers have a 'let out' for sermon preparation, relying solely on direct inspiration to speak out when they find themselves before a congregation. Intellectual sweat is undoubtedly a major part of sermon preparation for most preachers, alongside preparation in prayer. Undoubtedly God *could* preach through the lips of a person in a similar manner as the Holy Spirit sometimes gives utterance during prayer to those who have the gift of praying in tongues. God seems content, however, to make use of our limited understanding and intellectual achievements to fulfil this awesome ministry in conjunction or partnership with some kind of working of inspiration.

Inspiration without intellectual preparation, in general, seems lacking in 'meat'. Intellectual preparation without prayer and inspiration seems, in general, lacking in 'life'. Demarcation attempts between the two are doomed to failure. What one person understands as a God given inspired thought is another person's claim as human natural unconscious scanning. Indeed it *can* be argued that unconscious scanning is precisely God's 'inspiration' and in this case there is no need to postulate an external giving at all (external in the sense of the idea not originating within man), yet it is a bold and perhaps arrogant preacher who claims that that is solely the case.

Another useful example is that of healing. It is claimed that all healing comes from God, for pain, disease and death have no permanent part to play in the Kingdom of God, however many and various are the ways of healing. The medical profession itself acknowledges the complexity of the situation without any reference even being made to the spirit or psychic. The boundaries between the body and mind have become so blurred as to be practically no longer existent, and the health of the individual now has to be viewed in relation to the complete environment of the physical and mental realms that includes a person's spiritual beliefs.

An abdominal pain may be the direct influence of an elderly aunt whom the individual cannot 'stomach'. It may be physically explained by the constant irritation of the woman causing undue stress. This could mean more concentrated acids being produced that in turn produce the pain. Then again it could be that the individual masks or diverts the emotional 'pain' the aunt is causing, to be expressed in a more socially acceptable form of a stomach disorder. Even so, whatever the correct explanation may be, the healing also may be achieved by more than one method. The aunt may be 'removed' somehow or the acidity lowered by physical medicine. Again the mental stress may be relieved through sublimation or by some other natural outlet or even by a change in the relationship with the aunt by counselling techniques. All may work.

The healing situation is much more complicated when we introduce psychic and spiritual possibilities. We then can recognise that the stomach may possibly be affected directly by unseen forces or the psychosomatic effect relieved by suggestion through subconscious telepathic means rather than direct verbal communication. Instantaneous healing may occur by the power of God during prayer or the relationship changed and the stress removed if the love of God is more deeply experienced and allowed to come into the situation. All is possible.

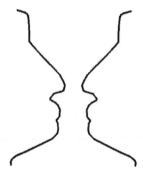

Where just two possible viewpoints can explain a situation this visual model expresses the argument best. The picture is a familiar one of just two lines, but these two lines and the space they define can be viewed in two ways. Either they are seen as two faces looking at each other or they may appear as a chalice. Some people see them one way, some the other way, or it is possible to see them in both ways and then to flick from one image to the other. What we are actually looking at are two curved lines but we interpret them or see them in different ways.

In a real life situation the two curved lines represent the observable facts, yet we may interpret these facts in more than one way. It may even be best to hold the differing explanations at the same time (flicking from image to image) to provide a better overall view of what is going on. Take, for example, an apparition that is 'seen'. In our example, one understanding may be that the person actually 'seeing' perceives an external entity not of the physical realms. Another, and perhaps a more generally held view, may be that the person 'seeing' is in such an abnormal mental state brought about by perhaps vitamin deficiency or malnutrition, exhaustion, drugs or alcohol that there is no external entity present and the apparition is nothing more than an hallucination. It is a figment of the imagination seen or interpreted by the brain in its abnormal state.

Either view may be quite legitimate on its own, but a combination of the two might possibly yield a further explanation. The person 'seeing' may in fact perceive an external entity, but only by the abnormal functioning of the brain in its abused or abnormal state. The features, clothing or substance of the apparition is given form by the person's innate clairvoyant faculty, past experiences, and personal, sociological and religious expectations. Otherwise it seems a bit bizarre to conclude that there is an apparent fashion in visions seen in different parts of the world. Mary is seen by Roman Catholics, Jesus by Protestants, Krishna by Hindus and colourful characters such as Monks, Lamas, Chinese, Native Americans etc. by Spiritualists and 'New Agers'!

The factors influencing a situation may thus be many and various, so the 'eyes may tend to rest' or the brain interpret more one view than another yet not necessarily dismissing one completely in favour of the other. Returning to the two-face line drawing, it may be that additional lines appear to be interpreted as eyes or hair which thus gives greater credence to one view than the other, but similarly circles may appear that can be interpreted as stones or gems on the stem or collar of the chalice. The different possible explanations of any given situation make it more complex to evaluate and give more options for subsequent action.

There is no such thing as a simple explanation!

26

What are the differences between Prayer, Meditation and Magic?

I thought it best to look at the differences between prayer, meditation and magic, for there is considerable confusion in people's minds about these three. They are not synonymous although there are areas of overlap. So let me begin first by speaking about prayer.

The exercise of prayer is an exercise of spirit. Of course it is an expression within the physical and also a use of the mental, but it is a spiritual exercise above all else. Unlike meditation or magic, prayer is essentially a state of being and not a point of doing.

Prayer is traditionally thought of as a dialogue with God, a pleading with God or an intercession with God. Usually there is not much in the way of silence and the mystic, and yet prayer is the state of mystical being.

The difference between speaking to someone else and speaking to God is not a matter of direction. You speak to someone who is out there, but you do not speak to God 'out there' unless it is more an act of superstition. It is also not just a matter of coming out with certain phrases or acts, for such a repeated act or ritual is no more than an empty outward action, unless there is some real inner meaning for the person praying within it. It is the same for repeated words or formularies. It is a waste of time to speak them unless there is meaning contained within the words for the speaker. The ritual will remain an empty act and the words will remain just a noise in the air, yet prayer is something much more than any of this. It is a state of 'being with God'; it is a recognising and an exercising of 'atonement with God', or a practising of 'being in the presence of

God'. These are all phrases that essentially mean the same thing, for it is something within the person, something that they are being rather than what they are doing, that constitutes praying.

If a sensitive or clairvoyant looks at someone who is praying and compares what they see with someone who is performing magic, then around the magician there should be seen lines of energy or forces at play, but around the person who is praying there may be nothing of this. There *could* be something, but more likely there may *not* be something, and that shows the difference between the two.

Yet one cannot divorce the spiritual exercise from the physical or the mental, for a person is a whole being. The physical body is usually involved with either a particular act or adopting an attitude of prayer or posture, and it is hoped that that is also true mentally. It may be the physical act of raising flags, or turning prayer wheels, or lighting candles, or burning incense. It may be looking into a flower or blade of grass, or an act of communion. In this situation, the repeated act is part of that prayer, as are the words or thoughts associated with it. However, it is the tuning into God, or invoking of God, or a looking towards God, (again, however you wish to describe it) that is essentially being in a relationship with God that turns the act or action into prayer. The praying can be an expression of thoughts of anguish, or peace, or beseeching, pleading, or praise. There may even be no words or thoughts at all, but it can all be part of prayer. In fact the deepest forms of prayer involve no words or thoughts at all but are just the acknowledgement of being in the presence of God – Being in God.

In that case a person can have a 'ministry of prayer' by holding up their heart's concerns to God. Because of their relationship with God there is an efficacious nature or a working out in some way of that prayer. Someone who has a great desire or concern, even if it were most laudable but does not have this relationship with God, may be just braying at the wind, a pouring out of their heart into the world around them. Of course God already knows their heart, but prayer is an act of *will* in the sense that the person actually chooses to pray, but it is essentially a spiritual exercise in that something of the spirit of that person is being with the Spirit of God.

That is not the case concerning Magic, although magic involves a person's spirituality. What is this person going to use the magic for? What of their emotional and spiritual maturity? Straightaway we can see that things of the spirit are involved with magic, but although magic is also above all else an act of will, it is a state of 'doing' rather than a state of 'being'.

Once more we see that there are physical things involved, such as stance, or a certain practice, or repeated act of ritual. There is also an attitude of mind, a tuning or preparation, as well as the spiritual aspects that I have just said, but magic is a using of a mental ability. It is a form of visualising. If a person cannot visualise, they cannot really perform magic, because in the act of visualising there is an energy flow. It may be a kind of direct line of sight phenomena or the visualising of a resonance that is taking place. It could be a focusing upon a chakra, an icon of some kind or a symbol, but it is essentially a deliberate and mental act.

There is one major possible misunderstanding concerning magic, for indeed a manual on magic is likely to say that first you have to 'be' in order to 'become'! This, however, is *not* 'being' in the sense that prayer uses the word, but of visualising or identifying with the situation in which the magic is needed. This is one reason why there is so much confusion with prayer. When thinking about magic, 'being' is really the wrong word to use. The meaning behind 'to be' in order 'to become', is that you 'be' that person you are identifying with, or you 'be' that object in the situation you desire. It is not a held *state* of being – 'being in the presence of God' as with prayer, but an active doing or 'changing into' or 'being' the object or target of your magic. You 'identify' with or 'be' the tree, or the creature, or the person of the magical situation, and in that understanding or acknowledgement of 'being' then you can 'become' what you desire, either by the sending of healing, or producing the miracle, or whatever it is. Prayer may invoke a desired action, but it is prayed that *God* will somehow fulfil the action, not the person praying.

Magic involves knowledge and the use of that knowledge. Prayer involves a relationship. So it is possible to have a person who is a very powerful magician, but with a low spirituality, who can still perform great magic – but it is not prayer. Similarly, you can have a person who has a tremendous prayer life, or vocation in prayer, but never seems to perform any miracles or magic at all. Ideally the two processes are present to some degree or other, for the magician may also be a person of prayer and hopefully the priest will have some magical abilities, even if they are subconscious. However, the magician may not be a priest and the priest may not be a magician.

Also take into account that the magician may take years to train, exercising for many, many hours over that time in order to become more proficient and a better or greater magician, but prayer is just being in the presence of God. You do not get 'better' at it. There is not a sense of earning anything in prayer as there is with magic, although there may be a discipline of time associated with it. However, you do not attain the status of Adept as a magician, unless you have trained, unless you have put tremendous discipline of work into your life, but you can be a person of prayer almost immediately, in the matter of faith and atonement.

So, what of meditation? Meditation is somewhere between the two. It is also an act of Will, but it is going beyond the thought and the thought processes, and approaching the things of spirit, of that relationship, through a mental technique. It is a quietening of the mind, alongside a quietening of the body. In that sense of quietening, it is not the anguished prayer or the beseeching prayer but it is the being still in prayer.

Meditation is not an act of magic, although it may focus on a chakra. It is not an act of prayer, although it may focus upon things that prayer uses, a flame, a flower, a chant or sound, a wheel or symbol. Meditation, by focusing gently upon that particular object or thought, is the process when thought disappears. You go through the symbol or the sound into a state of being, but it is not the same state of being alongside God as in prayer, rather than a particular mental state.

The most forgotten part of the meditation process is the coming out of meditation! This *is* part of the process and it is when a stray thought, a feeling of discomfort, a taste or a distraction brings the person back to normal thinking, and so recognising that they return to that point of focus, that mantra or icon. The relaxed going in and coming out of that mental state is meditation. It is not concentration, for that is hard work. It is not a trance state, for that is something yet again. It is a relaxed focusing that leads the mind beyond thought and back again, producing a profound physical and emotional state of relaxation and stability, opening the mind up to the reality that is all around, the reality of mind, body and spirit amongst the rest of creation and your place within it.

One last point in the working of meditation is that an attitude of mind can be held alongside the mantra, so that whilst meditating there is awareness or centring into the sacral chakra. If this is done, then as that chakra is mainly concerned with the emotions, there is a stabilising of the emotions and a forming of a strong emotional platform, which is most necessary if magic is to be seriously undertaken. Even if magic is never undertaken, this attitude cannot help but produce an emotional stability and so is surely a thing to be greatly desired.

There can be many different outward forms of prayer and there can be many different outward forms or systems of meditation, but the processes of both, although they both involve inward attitudes of awareness or 'being', are different. In meditation there is just the sense of being or centring within oneself, while with prayer it is the sense of being in the presence of God. Of course, God is everywhere and so God is within people who are meditating, but it is only in the sense that God is resting within the person. In prayer there is an active awareness of that presence, and so in this case it is the other way around in that the person in prayer is resting within the presence of God, even if the prayer is of anguish or lament!

When people misunderstand the process and say they are meditating when they are in fact praying with no thoughts, or just thinking prayerful thoughts, then it is most certainly not a meditation no matter how much they believe and tell others that they are. Similarly those who are meditating, if they say they are praying yet the process is not that of being in the presence of God, are meditating and not praying. Just because they say they are doing something does not make it so.

The exponent of the spiritual path will undoubtedly be a person of prayer. I hope they would also have times of meditation and quiet, and it would be wonderful if they also were able to exercise something of the gifts of magic. You can see how these processes overlap, for many a magical phrase may be said within the presence and awareness of God. Is that prayer or is it magic? When a person is meditating and in the stillness they find something of the God within, is that prayer or is it meditation? You can see how there can be these misconceptions, but essentially the three are separate practices.

It is all a complexity that demands understanding, patience and practice if you are going to work within the realms of the unseen. That is the life of a person who exercises the power of the sacred, be they Magician, Priest or Mystic.

27

The Question of Authority

Where lies Authority with regards to religion, spirituality and the power of the sacred?

To answer we should consider the different types of authority and weigh them one against the other before coming to any decision in matters spiritual. For example, time and again, especially in the New Age context, there is quoted the authority of Ancient Times. Where the information actually comes from is most certainly open to question but there are people who look back to a Golden Age of thousands of years ago, an age when everything was at its height and working so well. It was a time when it was a joy to be alive and participating in the work – which of course is a lot of nonsense. But still people look back as if the 'early factor' or just being spoken of as being old or stemming from a distant time – whether that claim is true or not – means the information has special authority. If the claim *is* true, then in one sense it does have an intrinsic authority for if it has stood the test of time there must be something worth retaining. It is only that time has taken a big leap through missing years – the information suddenly being found – then that argument must be put to one side and the claim investigated. However, if the claim is true then the teachings have been looked at, discussed, put into practice and pulled to pieces. If they have stood up to all those kinds of tests, then they must be worth looking at. So time can give Authority, but as society is always changing then just because something comes from long ago does not necessarily make it useful or of worth for today. There is no such time as a Golden Age that automatically validates all information supposedly stemming from that time which is good for all times to come.

You could actually call *this* time a golden age – an age of education and learning. There are more skills of discernment, of investigation, of academic appraisal of a situation with the worldwide system of communication than ever a society had in the past. Although all of that might be true and this is a Golden Age, somehow still I seriously doubt many of society's religious claims or justification for their use without great care!

Yet Age, the Test of Time, *is* one kind of Authority.

Take for example the gospels in the New Testament. Despite the apparent discrepancies the overall consensus upholds a general tenor. Discrepancies even support an academic integrity to authenticity of content that includes the age of the writings. If they were without such differences then doubt would be raised as to their source and age. We have the apparent eyewitness accounts with additional material in each that you would expect to find in any eyewitness account from different witnesses of any given situation. Too close a similarity would suggest collaboration. Too dissimilar an account would suggest that the account is in error or found distinctly wanting. Hence the latterly 'discovered' gospel according to Mary is particularly suspicious. Academic integrity is non-existent as it disagrees in fundamental ways and in basic principles to the New Testament gospels particularly as it is so recently 'found' with nearly 2,000 years' gap since its supposed writing. Indeed the 'Mary' claim is undoubtedly exposed as a ploy to age the writings and claim authority that it doesn't deserve.

The scriptures of any religion have an authority as they are the nearest records to the original teachings or actual events that gave rise to that religion. They may need investigation that questions the veracity of the writings but they hold an authority simply by their age and supposed source.

Another kind of authority, similar to that of time, is the authority invested by Tradition. I put it that way rather than calling it just a Corporate Nature of authority because tradition is not just being a corporate agreement at any one moment of time but being of a corporate nature *throughout* time. A tradition is something that has built up over the years, and although any writings or teachings might not have necessarily been encoded in a written form, they would have become encoded in a lore or ritual, a way of doing things passed on from person to person. In this agreed way there rests an authority. "We do it that way because we have always done it that way!", and change is always resisted, particularly with regards to religious practice.

The corporate voice has its own authority. I have already written about the power of peer pressure, but in its positive mode there is wisdom in the collective. It might change as fashion in thinking changes but hopefully the authentic voice of reason speaks through the babble in consensual reasoned thought. As I wrote before, it takes considerable strength for the individual to go against the many.

But then there is the authority of Conviction – if you know something is *right*, it has its own intrinsic authority. If you know something is true, you can still decide not to follow it or even go against it, because the practical situation dictates another course of action, but that inner feeling, that conviction, that ring of truth has its own authority and you will feel decidedly guilty about following any other direction. Ultimately, of course, it is this inner conviction that carries real weight accepting (or rejecting) other forms of authority, emphasising them, highlighting them or justifying them in some way – however you wish to put it. But that inner conviction, "it must be so", is what puts the seal on furthering one kind of authority over another – justifying its prominence and acceptance.

Some people give off an authority that they hold in their very demeanour. A person may have an 'air of authority' about them. In this case it is the personality, the charisma, which holds sway. It is not what is said but the way the person says it, the manner of it being said, that gives the sense of authority. There is that air about them that even if logical argument refutes their stance, still whatever they are saying has weight. That is the sheer power of charisma.

Then there is positional authority. For example, the person speaking may be a parent and a parent has authority over their child; a policeman has authority over other citizens; a priest has authority over their flock; an expert has an authority over a layman or non-expert in that field. The same is true concerning anyone in a position of acknowledged authority such as the high ranking soldier, the employer or the judge. A position that is recognised by others, indicated through uniform, law or some other similar insignia gives a degree of authority without any further words being spoken. It is that position which guarantees an authority whatever that person says, "Do this because I tell you to do so". Even so positional authority is linked to expertise.

Expertise holds the voice of experience and in some societies older people have an authority just because they are old. Because they speak with the voice of experience they must know what they are talking about for that expertise follows from a lifetime of learning. This is often formalised in various ways such as recognising degrees of understanding, especially if they have passed distinct examinations or levels of initiation. If that recognition is given by the corporate body of their particular scholastic or theological discipline, then others who are outside that particular corporate body can approach the person with a certain degree of confidence because they have a Master's Certification, or they have Passed the Abyss or they are called a Cardinal or whatever. Their expertise is acknowledged to the general people by their peers within that discipline. That is their authority.

But positional authority and expertise or experience has an authority of Might, which I have written about before. Power can be exercised in all sorts of ways, through money or through strength, through the policing, the forces, the rules and regulations. But who makes these rules and who puts them into practice? In the case of Law it is the Judge who hands out judgement according to rules made by those in Government. Both parties have authority and it is all an exercise of power. The magician, because he is able to do so, can exert his authority through means of magic. The healer or doctor, because he is seen to have power to heal, is given authority and respect by those he treats. But just because a person is experienced, is able and holds power in one field does not necessarily mean they are knowledgeable and should hold authority in others. There must always be discernment, a sorting out. What type of authority does this person hold? Do I accept what they say or not?

In particular there is the authority of Inspiration or channelling through the power of the sacred.

In Old Testament times, before anyone was accepted as a prophet, they had to be able to accurately give prophecy. It was not a matter of guessing correctly or being right 5 out of 6 times or even 9 out of 10. They had to be right 100 out of 100 times. They had to be right 100% and all of the time. Otherwise they were not recognised as being a prophet of God and could not utter those words, "Thus says the Lord!" Now that is an awesome requirement, an awesome level to attain and retain! Prophecy was real and accurate and Prophets held great authority. Their words were supposedly the actual Word of God.

Of a lesser degree are the words spoken by inspiration through a Channeller or Trance Medium. Words coming from the spiritual realms are deemed by many to hold special authority, simply because they are otherworldly. But just what is happening when a person channels information?

There are various factors which affect the message. The first one is in fact health. If the medium or channeller has a cold or is feeling unwell there is a difficulty in letting the subtle signals impinge. There is a 'fuzziness' to the exercise and it may be impossible to have a clear message. On the other hand, some forms of illness heighten sensitivity. There may be a physical disability or a psychological disability where compensation is that of greater sensitivity. In fact a sensitive person *is* often a physically weak person. Indeed, sometimes a sensitive deliberately seeks to become weakened through fasting, to the point of almost disability, to increase that sensitivity. The danger is that fasting could be taken to the extreme and at that point, rather than being an aid to sensitivity, the weakness could lead to hallucination – which of course is quite counterproductive.

Then there is the channeller's understanding of things, their intellectual ability, because the Communicator or communicating being uses the person's vocabulary and conceptualising ability to communicate. It is necessary to have a sensitive who is able to conceptualise well to get the message across. Specific terms now and again may not be a hindrance, but if the communicator is always struggling to find the concepts within the sensitive, then it is a thankless task.

If the sensitive is very easily overshadowed, it is possible to take most of their awareness of what is happening further away. It may even be possible to overshadow them so completely that, although there is difficulty sometimes in the translation, there is far more of the communicator's actual content and actual vocabulary present for the sensitive cannot interfere in any way. But even in this case there is still retained something of the channeller or medium which colours the message or *the kind* of message which is communicated. The theological and philosophical understanding of the medium and their deeper beliefs colours the message far more strongly than anything else. These pose a subtle but all pervasive constraint upon the communicator. So even if we take the medium far, far away in their mind, it may still prove to be impossible to say exactly what is wanted.

At this point the message is hedged with vague terms implying something which is untrue, or in the extreme situation containing outright untruths, because nothing else can be said, all in order to get perhaps just one real point across. It is like battling against the current of a stream or a river. If the stream wants to go in one direction and the being wants to channel it in another, then it may take an immense amount of force to do so. It may just be too much effort and be impossible to divert. Usually in channelling there is always the risk of not saying precisely what is required and of colouring the message by the messenger.

It would be so much easier if the being could simply say, "Thus says the Lord"!

There is the sad but sometimes amusing situation when the spirit communicator may have the misfortune of finding someone they can easily overshadow or communicate with, but they have in reality nothing to say! They just like opportunity to talk and delight in the mischievousness or sheer fun of communicating, or like the boost to their ego or image in doing this. Just because something comes through spirit does not mean to say it is of worth. Both the integrity of the channeller and the integrity of the communicator need to be taken into account when assessing the message's worth.

Any teachings should be able to stand up on their own. It should be obvious that what is being said is true because it can be validated again and again by anyone who has ability in that field. There should be a ring of truth about the words themselves, rather than because it is a spiritual source through this rather dubious means of communication. Some responsibility and discernment must rest with the person who is listening before accepting *anything*. To discern, to evaluate, to ascertain the truth in some way or other must be done. If the content is demonstrated – repeatedly demonstrated – to be correct, then when the message cannot easily be validated or it stretches acceptance, then authority may still be awarded.

Just because something claims to come from spirit, means that greater doubt should be put upon its authenticity because there are more factors which could influence it and rob it of its authority. As the writer of the Letters from John in the New

Testament puts it, 'test the spirits to see if they come from God', to acknowledge Jesus as being the Son of God – the Christ – and having been incarnate. And if they pass the test, the person on the receiving end should still be careful. There are many types of authority to hold against each other before accepting something as gospel.

28

So what is a way forwards for the Church in today's society?

One very obvious picture even now that is becoming ever clearer with the passing years is the death of the Church of England in its present form. The clergy are fighting a rearguard action as benefices are amalgamated, worshipping numbers rapidly decline and financial income disappears exponentially. Even should dioceses combine and the ordained Established ministry reflect a more Methodist approach, I wonder how many years are left before the last links between Church and State are finally broken and the C of E becomes a novelty group, sidelined to oddballs, religious throwbacks and theatre/media characters remembered with nostalgic affection and superficial concern.

And yet society, although now claimed to be a post Christian secular society, is far from being non-religious. Immigration may seem to have brought an influx of religious thinking and following to these shores but that is surely a tiny influence compared to what was already here, the evolving 'folk' religion that shows society's need to express 'something' at times of crisis, of mourning, or national awareness of tragedy, of sudden death, natural disaster, Remembrance, weddings (particularly of royal connection) and the like. And that 'something' includes a mystical, mysterious, spiritual element loosely embraced or personified by a Godlike being of unknown power, place or influence, be it benign or otherwise! There seems to be a religious gene somewhere in humanity's makeup. There seems to be a need for religious expression or understanding that is hotwired into the subconscious and pronounces its presence from time to time. Society, as an ever changing amorphous entity, cannot be without that religious element or spirituality that acknowledges the power of the sacred in some way or other. And if it is not portrayed through the Established Church or a major denomination, then what can that expression be?

The rise of the New Age philosophies resulted in a general revival of interest in pagan worship sites that went beyond their religious membership to include the general public. It gave a boost to tourism and heritage issues around and about these sites not seen in all the years of The National Trust's lifetime. Even the NHS suffered in unusual ways as Alternative Therapies gained ground and therapies such as hypnosis and acupuncture were allowed in hallowed NHS hospitals and clinics. Masters of this or that therapy are two a penny at New Age festivals, each claiming powers over and above those of their competitors and all pouring scorn on the traditional allopathic approach. New Ageism was a gift from the Gods for the feminist movement and the tree huggers and it became difficult, if not impossible, to dissociate things spiritual from things political or things of a gender issue. There was no clarity or voice of authority speaking when such a need was paramount. The Church had lost its unique position of being the giver of accepted spiritual wisdom as it spent all its energies on justifying ordination of women, new forms of worship and other navel gazing issues. And where ritual should be that expression of otherworldliness it also become a trap for the spiritually naive, it easily become a substitute for the real thing, for if the inner need is not fed then an ever increasing desperation to reclaim a lost 'something' demands further experimentation, new insights and a new approach to renew interest and an increase of worshipping attendees to prove the point.

Christianity is not dead, but the normal expression of that religion no longer does the business for most people in these lands. It is quickly becoming an expressionless religion with all the dangers inherent in that state. For where is the voice of authority when you need it? Where can a person go for that extra 'something' in time of need? Where is the collective wisdom if there is no collective anymore? Is superstition all that remains when there is no person with the respected charismatic or positional authority that was associated with the priests of past ages, even if it was eventually proven to be misplaced?

If the Church is to survive in some form or other then it needs to unashamedly state that religion is not simply a matter of feelings or justification by individuals claiming "The Lord is telling me to do this", or "My guides are telling me to do that". Sometimes anguish is part of exploring what is the way forwards for any individual, and pain that would rather be avoided by some form of such justification may be part of that person's crucifixion experiences in order to grow spiritually. The inner voices can be a most seductive trap and need to be held in tension with other wise words from elders or more spiritually mature confederates.

Christianity is a revealed religion in that it is the summation and interpretation of all that has gone before. It is not a 'once upon a time' religion and often has to accommodate within that interpretation uncomfortable developments in the real world of suffering, pain, disaster and political intrigue. God is not a thought experiment or a philosophy for the fireside. God is someone omnipotent, almighty, omnipresent and immortal who is held in relationship and separate from self. Understanding of God can only be touched upon by any one individual and only marginally more so when held corporately or collegiately. There needs to be an academic integrity alongside any understanding and voices of discussion or even dissent as interpretation and understanding is wrought forth.

In addition, although the Church has a ministry of conscience to the nation its prima facie existence is not in the political arena or even in social concern but in people's hearts and minds in order to express that inexpressible 'something'. That must come first.

Putting that together, I believe the way forwards for the

Church is to stop panicking about its 'materiel'. A 'mechanical' solution has been proven not to be the way to any kind of restoration, be that through revision of the priesthood – stipendiary or otherwise; the liturgy – forms of worship or use of projectors etc. or jiggling around with parish boundaries, combining benefices, and roles or even diocese. There needs to be a far more fundamental overhaul of what the Church is supposed to be presenting at the heart of its gospel and pastoral ministry. There needs to be almost a revolution within the powers that be and also found within the 'professional' Christian for the Church to be relevant and authoritative. And that will not come without heartache and much soul searching and possible dissenting clamour. The 'religious' way has not worked, for the Church is obviously dying. The power of the sacred is not really much in evidence at the moment within its walls. Spirituality, not only for the individual church member and priest but also for the corporate identity, must be reborn to challenge the spiritual darkness and ignorance of our society.

29

Practical Ways Forward

A revolution does not have to be heralded by a mighty explosive event. Indeed the most profound revolutions usually come quietly from the very members of the institution that is under reform. In fact, in my view the best revolutions come about when the institution is not even aware that a revolution has taken place! Members wake up to that change one day only when it has been pointed out by one of their more astute members. This is the kind of change that enters by the back door that I suggest could happen within the Church – with careful planning and gentle introduction of small changes nudged into place by those in the know.

If the institution is fighting a losing battle then what is the last line of defence? Given the ordained ministry is going to be evermore dependent upon the non-stipendiary or volunteer ministry then where should the vanishing stipendiary priesthood best be placed?

I have argued before that perhaps diocesan positions rather than parish ones should be 'consolidated' by amalgamating with neighbouring areas to save salaries, rather than continue with the self-defeating practice of combining benefices to the extent that a single stipendiary priest is often in charge of an area that used to be normally associated with an entire deanery. Instead of retaining each diocesan administrating machinery with its non-productive (business sense of the word) workforce but keeping more of the finance at the parish coalface, it would maximise the manpower at the parish level where it rightfully belongs. That would mean at least redefining administrative areas for these need not necessarily coincide with present diocesan ones. It would mean combining many diocesan roles that take time and resources away from the parish level. As with business, the non-productive workforce can so easily grow to manage ever increasing bureaucratic piles of paper, but once in place it is near impossible to downsize the administration without a major upheaval, as can be seen in the statutory bodies, nationalised industries and state run NHS. It calls for very strong leadership to call the bluff of the administrators and return the financial focus to the practical workers where it truly belongs.

On the other hand cathedrals, by their historic influence and geographical positions, have an undoubted prominence that cannot be ignored. Whether they continue to coincide with the historic diocesan see is another matter – what's in a name? I don't see why they necessarily should. Just as benefices can be combined so can dioceses, but that doesn't mean that the central sociological position of a cathedral should be left to decline into museum status if a diocese ends up with more than one cathedral. They are natural centres of activity, and hopefully that activity would be in the best interest of the Church as a spiritual centre of note. Most cathedrals still have an underlying atmosphere of prayerful activity and hint at the power of the sacred, especially when no one is around! Indeed most have been built on pre-Christian worship sites that have employed the partially understood geomantic properties of ley lines to enhance that very power. It would be foolishness to throw away such an asset simply because of dwindling resources, despite their apparent financial drain.

Many priests have no psychic sensitivity and see no value in the existing worship buildings. They have no appreciation of the legacy of hundreds of years of prayer in such places and the effect that this has on the atmosphere, mystery and sacred power contained within them. It is a truly wonderful treasure of the unseen power that a previous religious priesthood not only understood but manipulated (probably ritually) for the good of the community. It cannot be perceived by physical eyes alone. Insensitivity sees only the financial black hole before them.

Cathedrals in particular incline themselves to centres of excellence, of seats of authority, tradition, grandeur and the sacred. Surely such places can house education and learning and become examples of the exercise of sacred power through times of ritual, healing prayer, different types of healing, meditation, lectures and study of the traditionally esoteric arts (!!), for from such comes the public acclaim of recognition in this spiritual arena, of meeting the challenge of the New Age philosophies, of standing up for the Christian gospel and the treasures of Christ's teachings in scripture. Without personalities necessarily being in the forefront, the cathedrals would reclaim the central position of interest and authority on all things sacred.

There is no reason why cathedrals could not invite alternative practitioners to hold therapy sessions somewhere within the cathedral close or actual cathedral building and so ensure a connection and controlling influence with the more accepted and respected practices. There is no reason why cathedrals could not mount workshops, courses or even conferences on various aspects of healing, arcane knowledge and holistic well-being. Even though the visiting lecturers might promulgate ideas divergent from the Christian ideal, their views remain their own with appropriate disclaimers from the Church, but it would be the Church that would be gradually recognised as being a front runner in the power of the sacred rather than the Alternatives, meeting the challenge of the New Age and gradually acknowledging its own expertise in these fields. It would certainly stretch Christian apologists and help people of all persuasions to examine their beliefs and spiritual practices.

Above all, cathedrals should be the venue for continual or regular contemplative prayer and meditation, and exercise their traditional role of upholding this mystery of mystic practice rather than rely on the set service times of public worship.

The cathedrals are too fine an asset to waste in limiting their activity to ritual alone.

30

Practice of the Power of the Sacred – Corporately

The site itself

Pre-Christian worship sites were not chosen simply because of their proximity to a population centre but more because of the peculiar properties of the land in that place. In fact I am sure that there are examples of it being the other way around, of population growing because of the worship site. Either for a predilection towards health or fecundity or towards the manipulation of power over the environment, the geomantic strengths of the place were utilised by ritual and enhanced through shape and materials to produce a site that had to be set aside for no other purpose but to exercise the power of the sacred. As a consequence many of the sites grew in significance, size and authority so that although today we still have the awesome places such as Stonehenge, Avebury, Castlerigg and the like, many of the lesser sites such as Mên-an-Tol, the Hurlers and numerous stone circles still retain an aura of mystery and power.

Many such sites were Christianised during the evangelising of the land, for why waste a good worship site and practice habit. Thus many churches and cathedrals were built on pre-Christian foundations. Of course the greatest of these pre-Christian sites such as Avebury were too eminent, large or established to take over and build upon but the majority, especially those near population centres, could easily be revamped and dedicated to Christian saints for the habit of worship already resided there.

More importantly the power of the sacred still resided in the stones and very land, so despite a major change of theological direction many of the sought outcomes of differing prayer and practice were still the same and utilised the same unseen subtle energies of such places, possibly unwittingly.

Prayer is a power as well as a discipline of the spiritually minded, and like any muscle that is trained to be used wisely it grows in spiritual strength the more it is practiced. That is just as true for a corporate identity as for an individual. So the more a body of believers exercised prayerfully and with certainty, the aura of power was more deeply impressed upon the place and consequently felt. Hence the suggestion of continual prayer or meditation at any site of natural sacred power is not just a nice idea or thought experiment.

There is nothing like success to breed further success so naturally the more politically powerful centres were bound to grow into places of religious pre-eminence. So abbeys, monasteries and cathedrals grew in prominence and power.

Now, however, is the time to re-evaluate the use of such physical resources, but in ways that would not cause a great upheaval or a blare of trumpets announcing that change to the world.

The priesthood involved in the sites

All the words in the world are of no worth unless the truth held behind the words is felt as well as being capable of standing up to critical inspection. Authority is only awarded in these days of the personality cult when the person can actually and repeatedly deliver the goods. Otherwise the authority is withheld by the general public, no matter what claims are made or what position that person making a claim may hold within an institution. Hence the need for that initial presentation to be without hype and vacillation, and to be obviously sincere and meaningful – and for real. It is time indeed for the priesthood to be steeped in knowledge and ability of the unseen powers that they pertain to uphold.

A religion that doesn't deliver would quickly be resigned to the scrapheap. All hot air and liturgical theatre will not replace the feeling of truth contained in religion when practiced by those with true authority.

31

Practice of the Power of the Sacred – Individually

It is an indictment of the priesthood that so few clergy can sense the reality behind the words, gestures and thoughts of the services that they themselves conduct.

There are many different gifts and talents that any society or group utilise – and of course the church is no exception. Some people are born administrators, others make great pastors, others still are orators or evangelists, others teachers or financial wizards. All have come together in the past as a team to enable the church to exist or even thrive over the years. But in today's atmosphere of rekindled interest in the things of subtle energies alternative spiritualities, religious thinking and practice, it is important for the church to present the gifts of the spirit, not as part of a charismatic specialist worship group like the Evangelicals or Anglo-Catholics, but as a regular part of the ordained ministry, having no special affiliation to any group within the church. Such gifts must be able to be recognised by the Alternatives and measured up against. In other words psychic abilities should be fostered and not deplored. They should be part of the practice of the power of the sacred. They should be used and not feared by the church. Within the context of the church there is a wisdom and safety for such gifts to be employed alongside all the other gifts that build up the body of believers.

There is no reason for not reintroducing the very ancient practice of teaching and training people in the use of such gifts in esoteric schools rather than leaving individuals with the most dangerous task of discovering their abilities by trial and error, hiding the use of such from colleagues and friends because of the witch hunt mentality of the majority. There is no reason why they cannot be openly used within the Ministry of Deliverance, showing understanding and ability way, way above that of superstitious dread and ritualistic theatre and 'magic' that is currently the main offering in this area of the church's work. These things should be embraced by the whole church and not just by the Church's Fellowship for Psychical and Spiritual Studies. That particular group needs not be a society for the strange-thinking churchman. Indeed most church people are not aware that such a group actually exists within the Church of England! But it has been working in the background for many years. It is only when the profile of the esoteric has been raised and generally accepted in the church that the challenge of the Alternatives can be met and the authority of the Church restored in the area of spiritual knowledge, power and ability.

Security and ability in these areas grow like any other gift when exercised. However, what can also be seen is the effect of prayer, healing gifts and any exercise of the power of the sacred upon the practitioners' spirituality. The direct relationship that exists between emotional maturity and spiritual maturity or spirituality cannot be ignored. It is part of the 'guarantee' that St Paul writes about concerning the work and fruit of the Spirit. It is a direct consequence of practicing the presence of discipleship in the area of life that relies on faith and the power of God as against just the power of individuals in the realms of spiritual forces and spiritual warfare.

Example is the only true persuader – not logic or argument.

32

Conclusion

The Church of England, if it follows its present practice of 'consolidation' or amalgamation of parishes, has only a few more years before it collapses in moribund bankruptcy. The leadership numbers alone speak volumes, for over the 40 years since I was ordained it has shrunk by seventy-five per cent. Money is drying up and cathedrals are desperate for finance just to maintain the fabric. Parish churches cannot possibly afford major repairs and buildings are being left to decay or sold off, following the example of the nonconformist worshipping communities. Despite the historic central position that the Church has enjoyed in UK society over the last thousand years and the respect that its clergy have been shown it cannot survive without manpower and money unless a revolution in presentation takes place. It begs the question that if God truly is the guiding hand behind the Church then where the hell is He taking it?

The answer, I believe, is, of course, that the Church is all too human an institution that at present has lost its way. Whether God truly guides the Church is a matter of faith and debate but I think there is time for the Church to wake up to its prophetic ministry concerning this nation's spiritual paucity and declining standards of respect, integrity and national pride and still do something about it. At the moment it does not present a relevant message or appreciative ministry that people relate to, for if it did then church attendance would reflect that as a direct consequence. The subsequent greater membership would yield a larger pool to draw upon for future leadership and income would grow in proportion.

When looking further than the Christian expression in these lands, although we live in a multi-faith country, the only other intrinsically historic religion in the UK is that of the New Age. Unfortunately it has experienced what amounts to a break of identity during the last fifteen hundred years or so, so despite its claims to the contrary it can no longer be considered a 'High' religion. In fact rather than being a distinct religion at all, the New Age is best described as a movement, for it is more a collection of individuals without a cohesive quality. It has no collective authority or obvious spokesperson. It is an amorphous conglomerate of widely varying teachings where 'masters' who have the loudest voice or most colourful presentation win the acclaim in their locality of like-minded people.

For the vast majority of the populace in the UK the Church is totally irrelevant – something to be trotted out for funerals, possibly Remembrance, possibly Christmas and possibly weddings. But that is all! To be blunt about it I have heard it voiced by people outside of either group that the Church is the walking dead with a few congregations hanging on denying the death throes of the whole institution. At the same time the general populace, I am sure, tends to regard the New Agers with deep scepticism or even ridicule, consigning adherents as minority cliques of tree huggers, extreme feminists, spaced out or stoned meditators or weirdly dressed zany zealots living in fairy land on the benefit system.

Hopefully neither description of the respective groups is true but it seems to me that if either the Church or the New Age had any real relevance or obvious treasure that the rest of society could value then the picture would be very different and spirituality would not be a thing for the tiny minority to investigate or desire. Certainly the Church tends to regard the New Age as a seductive trap set by the darker forces in the world and the New Age looks to the Church as a prehistoric institution responsible for untold outrages against the Old Religion adherents and spiritually vulnerable loners who could not bring themselves to dissemble and seek anonymity amongst the mainstream religious.

Yet between them these two groups of people possess resources, enthusiasm, talent, gifts, tremendous breadth of teachings and understanding that should take them beyond the accusations of the generally spiritually dense and bridge the gap of the battle of the sexes that they epitomise in their respective ways, one representing Mother Earth Goddess and the other Sky Father God. If each could bring themselves to respect the other sufficiently to explore a working relationship then an experiential and exciting possibility arises. It wouldn't be a united voice but at least it would be a combined voice speaking about things of the spirit.

Churches, particularly cathedrals and those built on ley lines, contain the legacy of sacred power and could become known as centres of therapy and of healing if the resources could be shared in some way. The geomantic properties of the old buildings and worship centres could not help but enhance the effectiveness of most forms of therapy practiced by many of the New Age practitioners. The Church would ultimately benefit as its voice would once again be heard in the arena of spiritual dialogue but in the local community rather than any political scenario or social crusade depicted in the media – heard where it counts amongst the people it is supposed to serve. While the New Age adherents would benefit with the use of facilities steeped in prayer and spiritual power, giving an efficacy to their therapies and meditation not experienced in their separate rooms or shrines.

It does not mean that anyone would have to give up their beliefs – far from it, or lose their faith (heaven forbid) in the working relationship but the authority of the Church would be challenged, and that is not a bad thing at all. Out of such association together belief would be re-evaluated. Dialogue and discussion might show discomfort and initial hostility with varied teachings and leadership but it would sharpen everyone's ideas about the things of the spirit. The overall help to the community through direct hands-on therapy and daily prayer would hopefully result in a developing respect from the community for both groups. A platform would be almost accidentally offered to voice concern for the environment and the dangers of pollution and climate change, which both groups of people pay more than lip service to. Similarly, respect for things feminine as well as masculine could not be dodged as well as respect for charismatic authority and acceptance of spiritual power beyond the mundane and physical. The relevance of all things spiritual would become obvious and yet be at the very centre of modern daily life and living. That would be Spirituality Reborn.

There is nothing sacred about the Church and its Christian expression as history shows, but there is every reason to hope for its continued well-being in some other form or other. There is potential for growth for those whose spiritual eyes have been opened to the wonders all around them, potential for those who have been truly 'born again' of whatever persuasion but who do not necessarily conform to any promulgated dogma or constitution of faith.

I can only pray that it happens.

CHRISTIAN
ALTERNATIVE

THE NEW OPEN SPACES

Throughout the two thousand years of Christian tradition there
have been, and still are, groups and individuals that exist in the
margins and upon the edge of faith. But in Christianity's
contrapuntal history it has often been these outcasts and
pioneers that have forged contemporary orthodoxy out of
former radicalism as belief evolves to engage with and
encompass the ever-changing social and scientific realities. Real
faith lies not in the comfortable certainties of the Orthodox, but
somewhere in a half-glimpsed hinterland on the dirt track to
Emmaus, where the Death of God meets the Resurrection,
where the supernatural Christ meets the historical Jesus, and
where the revolution liberates both the oppressed and
the oppressors.

Welcome to Christian Alternative... a space at the edge where
the light shines through.
If you have enjoyed this book, why not tell other readers by
posting a review on your preferred book site. Recent bestsellers
from Christian Alternative are:

Bread Not Stones
The Autobiography of An Eventful Life
Una Kroll
The spiritual autobiography of a truly remarkable woman and a
history of the struggle for ordination in the Church of England.
Paperback: 978-1-78279-804-0 ebook: 978-1-78279-805-7

The Quaker Way
A Rediscovery
Rex Ambler
Although fairly well known, Quakerism is not well understood.
The purpose of this book is to explain how Quakerism works as
a spiritual practice.
Paperback: 978-1-78099-657-8 ebook: 978-1-78099-658-5

Blue Sky God
The Evolution of Science and Christianity
Don MacGregor
Quantum consciousness, morphic fields and blue-sky
thinking about God and Jesus the Christ.
Paperback: 978-1-84694-937-1 ebook: 978-1-84694-938-8

Celtic Wheel of the Year
Tess Ward
An original and inspiring selection of prayers combining
Christian and Celtic Pagan traditions, and interweaving their
calendars into a single pattern of prayer for every morning
and night of the year.
Paperback: 978-1-90504-795-6

Christian Atheist
Belonging without Believing
Brian Mountford
Christian Atheists don't believe in God but miss him: especially
the transcendent beauty of his music, language, ethics, and
community.
Paperback: 978-1-84694-439-0 ebook: 978-1-84694-929-6

Compassion Or Apocalypse?
A Comprehensible Guide to the Thoughts of René Girard
James Warren
How René Girard changes the way we think about God and the
Bible, and its relevance for our apocalypse-threatened world.
Paperback: 978-1-78279-073-0 ebook: 978-1-78279-072-3

Diary Of A Gay Priest
The Tightrope Walker
Rev. Dr. Malcolm Johnson
Full of anecdotes and amusing stories, but the Church is still a
dangerous place for a gay priest.
Paperback: 978-1-78279-002-0 ebook: 978-1-78099-999-9

Do You Need God?
Exploring Different Paths to Spirituality Even For Atheists
Rory J.Q. Barnes
An unbiased guide to the building blocks of spiritual belief.
Paperback: 978-1-78279-380-9 ebook: 978-1-78279-379-3

The Gay Gospels
Good News for Lesbian, Gay, Bisexual, and Transgendered
People
Keith Sharpe
This book refutes the idea that the Bible is homophobic and
makes visible the gay lives and validated homoerotic
experience to be found in it.
Paperback: 978-1-84694-548-9 ebook: 978-1-78099-063-7

The Illusion of "Truth"
The Real Jesus Behind the Grand Myth
Thomas Nehrer
Nehrer, uniquely aware of Reality's integrated flow, elucidates
Jesus' penetrating, often mystifying insights – exposing
widespread religious, scholarly and skeptical fallacy.
Paperback: 978-1-78279-548-3 ebook: 978-1-78279-551-3

Do We Need God to be Good?
An Anthropologist Considers the Evidence
C.R. Hallpike
What anthropology shows us about the delusions of New
Atheism and Humanism.
Paperback: 978-1-78535-217-1 ebook: 978-1-78535-218-8

Fingerprints of Fire, Footprints of Peace
A Spiritual Manifesto from a Jesus Perspective
Noel Moules
Christian spirituality with attitude. Fourteen provocative
pictures, from Radical Mystic to Messianic Anarchist, that
explore identity, destiny, values and activism.
Paperback: 978-1-84694-612-7 ebook: 978-1-78099-903-6

**Readers of ebooks can buy or view any of these
bestsellers by clicking on the live link in the title. Most
titles are published in paperback and as an ebook.
Paperbacks are available in traditional bookshops. Both
print and ebook formats are available online.**

**Find more titles and sign up to our readers' newsletter at
http://www.johnhuntpublishing.com/christianity
Follow us on Facebook at
https://www.facebook.com/ChristianAlternative**